Selected and New Poems

BY THE AUTHOR:

POETRY
Time Without Number
Encounters
The World for Wedding Ring
No One Walks Waters
False Gods, Real Men
Trial Poems (with Tom Lewis)
Selected and New Poems

PROSE
The Bride
The Bow in the Clouds
They Call Us Dead Men
Consequences: Truth and . . .
Love, Love at the End
Night Flight to Hanoi
No Bars to Manhood
The Trial of the Catonsville Nine
The Geography of Faith (with Robert Coles)
The Dark Night of Resistance
America Is Hard to Find
Absurd Convictions, Modest Hopes (with Lee Lockwood)
Jesus Christ (with Gregory and Deborah Harris)

Selected
and New Poems

DANIEL BERRIGAN

DOUBLEDAY & COMPANY, INC.
Garden City, New York   1973

ISBN: 0-385-03099-1 TRADE
0-385-03088-6 PAPERBOUND
LIBRARY OF CONGRESS CATALOG CARD NUMBER 72-118847
COPYRIGHT © 1973 BY DANIEL BERRIGAN
PRINTED IN THE UNITED STATES OF AMERICA
FIRST EDITION

811
B - 6.95 6/7/74 ©

Acknowledgment is made to the following for permission to reprint their material: Most of the poems in this volume were previously published in the following books by The Macmillan Company: *False Gods*, copyright © 1967, 1968, 1969 by Daniel Berrigan, S.J.; *No One Walks Waters*, copyright © Daniel Berrigan 1966; *Time Without Number*, copyright © Daniel Berrigan 1952, 1957; *World for Wedding Ring*, copyright © Daniel Berrigan 1958, 1959, 1960, 1961, 1962. Reprinted by permission of The Macmillan Company.

"Abraham" and "Saint Stephen" first published in *The Commonweal*; "Saint John Baptist" and "Snowman" first published in *Poetry* magazine; "Saint John Baptist I," "Saint Peter," and "Tree: October" first published in *Spirit* magazine; "Saint Joseph II," "Saint Ann," and "Lazarus" first published in *Thought* magazine; "Abel," "Christ," "Atlas," "Apostles," "Thirst," "Hear Ever So Gently," "Men Were the Image," "More Like the Sea," "Child Above a Flower," "An Old Woman in Death," "Vocation," "We Love," and "Go Down on Knee," all poems taken from *Encounters* by Daniel Berrigan. Copyright © 1960 by The World Publishing Company. Reprinted by permission of The World Publishing Company.

"1969 Opened Like This," "At the Time of His Death, Americans Had Mastered the Dynamics of a Moon Flight," "Edifying Anecdotes Concerning the Deceased Are Now in Order," "Memories After the Fact: A Visit of Ill-favored Characters to the Monastery," and "Who's Who at the Obsequies" appeared in Volume 7, Number 2, Summer 1969 issue of *Continuum* magazine.

"Arrival" and "Torment" from *No Bars to Manhood* by Daniel Berrigan. Copyright © 1970 by Daniel Berrigan. Reprinted by permission of Doubleday & Company, Inc. "Wings," "The Marshal," "John Urey," "Guilty," "A Typical Day in the Municipal Zoo," "Eucharist," "The Boxes of Paper Ash," and "The Verdict" taken from the book *Trial Poems* by Daniel Berrigan. Text of poetry copyright © 1970 by Daniel Berrigan, S.J. Reprinted by permission of Beacon Press.

THANK YOU EVERYONE UP TO NOW/ David Darst fire eater/ Dowds for white ducks/ Connett for Biafra hope/ Danielou (formerly)/ Betti's Inspector; "you'll have to dig your way out of this mess alone"/ Paul Naomi Maria Peter/ OM/ Cross Currents/ 3 evergreens planted at Danby after 3 deaths/ Grady's laugh, Teresa's silence/ Colorado mountain flowers/ Congdon's crucifixion/ Merton be with us./ South African chief's bead necklace/ the model village privy from Hanoi/ Hudson River coming back/ my father's hands, dying/ a paper Christmas star cut from a draft delinquency notice/ Tony Walsh, Labre House/ Chavez/ Song My, My Lai people (forgive us)/ Goss-Meyrs/ Year One/ Al Uhrie murdered/ The Sacred Heart Program/ Dr. Josef Smolek, Comenius Faculty, Jungmannova 9, Prague, Czechoslovakia (as far as anyone knows)/ Jack St. George, those memories!/ David Miller, Cathy, you showed the way/ Quigleys of course and Lambs/ Paul and Ed and the Peruvian kid's baptism/ Tony Meyer yes/ Rocco and his brother and sister/ Paul & Polly Gibbons/ the isle of Iona/ Marymount/ Philip thank you/ Mother Pauline and the sea shells/ the Preyres of Tanger/ Stevie, Cotter, Davis, Niz, that good fellowship/ Nhat Hanh; show us his glory./ Estelle for the Lao flute/ 4 Graystones/ Paul Cowan, the truth is out/ Jeremy for going and coming/ Jock Vanier and the crippled children/ Flavin Fitzgibbons Frains/ Gerry, Mary, the tie dye shirt/ Sister Josephine arise/ Nelly for fraises and the apocalyptic bird/ Mel, Elizabeth/ hey there Pat Farren pass the bread/ Père Charmot free standing strength/ Freddy for making light/ Packard Manse go further please/ Dixie what a smile girl/ thank you Seidenbergs/ Ernest and Bertel play the violin and smile/ Groppi make it/ Roger LaPorte for dying for us/ Karl Meyer don't pay/ Corita color/ Dorothy Day, live a thousand years/ Fred Pomeroy come back/ Everyone at Immaculate Heart/ John Deedy doughty/ to olive oil/ Parrilla and the prisoners/ Heidbrinks/ Zinns my kins/ 3 pilots sprung/ Stevensons all/ Abraham Heschel rest in Abraham./ Warden Foster Baltimore County jail/ Joe Pizza free man/ J. Edgar Hoover, his new year encyclical/ Judge Thomsen/ the oracles, my wooden whale/ Resisters all/ Tom's flag destroyed, children not for burning/ Bob and Mig Hoyt, founder and found/ Bill and Tony and the Block Island swans/ Integrity mag/ the Golden Gate bridge on foot/ the G. Washington bridge on foot/

the Red River pontoon bridge by car/ some Jesuits/ Joe, Mary Ellen for cutting loose/ Ivan Illich/ Eqbal and Julie and wonder child/ Peter Blouin and the bleeding corner/ bullpens I have paced in/ Betty Bartelme always there/ Freda & all 6/ the internal revenue service for laughs/ Six Mile creek/ Slowhawk Airlines for surprises/ Hyannisport/ El Monton/ pot/ Buchman Kunstler Freeman and Cunningham/ El Greco/ Picasso for looking like Merton/ 1 black federal marshal name unknown, thank you/ Allenwood *Waupun*/ Rebel Yell Bourbon/ homemade napalm (inquiries invited) yurt commune dwellers/ Goldmans Finlays Jean and Jim/ Norman, Gebby and the shoe last Norse God/ Jerryknoll/ the dancing bear on rue Madame/ Copacabana beach, my stolen trousers/ gospel of St. Matthew, cc 5–8/ Lake Champlain, a cabin in August/ Paraclete take wings/ George Justus for being omniman/ Izzy Stone for standing there/ Joyce/ Rambusch's postcards, for keeping arriving/ Hamilton school/ la Lettre/ Rafael/ Harry Stevens, gone and come back/ Wilsons on a farm somewhere/ Srs. Marcella, Rose, Lua you started something/ Madame Salsamundi believing and dying/ McGovern's artists/ Schlacter eating kosher, loving the goys/ everyone around curw keep saying it/ Shadowbrook for the prayer rug/ West 98 Street Jesuits and the next move/ NY *Times* playing it safe/ Ciciones love you/ both my grandmothers/ the lives (and deaths) of children/ Clem listening all night/ Village Haven, Theresa Jean/ Tom Lewis, the art of prison/ the birds on Santa Barbara beaches, come mourn with me/ Gary Comstock, Bruce Dancis you spoke up/ Zahn and Jagerstätter/ Matty Goodman, Paul Goodman, good men/ Walshes/ everyone in Montreal, Pueblo, West Point Mississippi and Upper Tupper Lake/ East Hill School/ the Half (defunct), the Ithaca Seed Company/ death row, San Quentin/ Jews who mourn and move with us/ Ann Walsh, the Irish poncho/ Vietnam Friends, an end of agony/ AmerIndians Polynesians Quakers Sufis Tibetans Zens Bushmen Witches Yogis Druids Taoists Catholics. poets innumerable/ all natural orders/ John and the rock Mass/ Tim Dimock and the wooden necklace/ James Pike these bones shall live/ Bill Guindon keeping hands off/ Pham Van Dong for roses at Christmas/ the Milwaukee 14, separate but equal/ Iron Mt. and the cure of souls/ the Human Being lawn mower/ AJ Muste no graveyards no end in sight/ the FBI for dropped jaws/ Berchmans/ Mary Newland and the tree of life/ Macarius, the monks, the fruit cake/ Pope John for dying young/ Helder Camara what a man might be/ Anne and Vi/ nieces and nephews lead kindly light/ Most of us, the long run/ Gary

Snyder, the smoky the bear sutra/ Ken Feit, the liberated ice cubes/ the day we burned the hunting licenses/ Alcatraz/ Gordon and Judy and the nightingales/ OK Flora/ Leland stay young with us/ Jesus the price of being man/ Jim Forest I see the trees/ Danbury & a near burial/ Bread and Puppets, we made it!/ Liberation News Commune/ the Claremont Christians coffee at all hours/ Ellul, the truth is bearable, barely/ Dublin and the soft rain/ Bill Dych for making the move/ Breyderts, the grace of living/ all at the *Catholic Worker*, the constant vision/ amen alleluia

CONTENTS

I. *Time Without Number*

II. *Encounters*

III. *The World for Wedding Ring*

IV. *No One Walks Waters*

VI. *Trial Poems*

Selected and New Poems

I

TIME WITHOUT NUMBER

STARS ALMOST ESCAPE US

They come unwilling
to greatness, unlike dramatic trees
in chorus, miming man's destiny
with want and plenty, with grinning or tragic
masks.

Size makes no difference. Nor have stars taken
easily to being something other. Their blossoming
momentarily in hedges, depends on a man's
stillness: let him come near, and the doe's eye leaps,
the fireflies leap into a thicket or heaven.

You may decline a whole night of stars
by lighting or snuffing a candle in a closet.
Not one, or all their sum of light taken together,
can keep a stranger's feet on his tricky road.

For what then?
the true, the beautiful, struggles
in winds and spaces, and scarcely, perilously wins

BIRTHDAY IN QUEBEC
(*eighty-six*)

I

I remember today a roadside, the crucifix
raised crude as life among farming people,
its shadow creeping, dawn and twilight, over their lives.
Among wains, haycocks and men it moved like a savior.

So old, so scored by their winters, it had been staked out
perhaps by a band of ruffians on first Good Friday.
The way it endured, time would have bruised his fist in striking it.

What time had done, breaking the bones at knee and wrist,
washing the features blank as quarry stone,
turning the legs to spindles, stealing the eyes

was only to plant forever its one great gesture
deeper in furrow, heave it high above rooftops.

Where time had done his clumsy worst, cracking its heart,
hollowing its breast inexorably,—he opened this Burning-glass
to hold the huge landscape: crops, houses and men, in Its fire.

II

He was irremovably there, nailing down the landscape,
more permanent than any mountain time could bring down
or frost alter face of. He could not be turned aside
from his profound millennial prayer: not by birds
moved wonderfully to song on that cruel bough:
not by sun, standing compassionately at right hand or left.

Let weathers tighten or loosen his nails: he was vowed to stand.
Northstar took rise from his eyes, learned constancy of him.
Let cloudburst break like judgment, sending workmen homeward
whipping their teams from field, down the rutted road to barn

4

still his body took punishment like a mainsail
bearing the heaving world onward to the Father.

And men knew nightlong: in the clear morning he will be there,
not to be pulled down from landscape, never from his people's
        hearts.

EVERYTHING THAT IS

                          is not something other:
a ridiculous pablum for the poet's mind
until the wind sing it, or star bring it
ringing its name through the astonished night:

or on a March day, the crocus
struggle into air.
                          Or the autumn maple *glory! glory!*
puzzle the strollers with its identical form
four months later assumed again.
                        Such things shake the mind
backward, inward:
                I wonder who knew the stars
from flowers, before flowers were not stars:
before trees spread
               between one and other
        a growth
by night starlike, by day a flowering?

And yet itself

ITS PERFECT HEART

It was November: an invisible fire
freshened the heart of the grey-blue heron
that had drifted and loved contented
on mild streams, among summer dwellings and children.

But what aroused it powerfully
that it shook earth like a disease, pettiness and location,
to set breast against wearying universal air?

Now while dawn streams upward from fields
or early stars send man to fireside
still it labors above him, by day and night
starting the sunrise, shadowing the red leaning moon;

sufficient, remote from the longings of men
as they look aloft: vowed to greatness
and powerfully steered by its lodestone, its perfect heart.

THE MOON

This desolate cold god
never created a flower
in his salty furrow,
or called noble birds to climb
and drink at his vein of fire:

he never walked the noon
alight with his own light
whose trees were his sudden fountains
whose waterfalls stood and shouted:

but shod and ribbed in ice
he keeps heart averted
from the plague of youth, from growth:

he has sworn his cold eye
never will heat or approve
the blood that rounds man's breast
and grows the fruit hung there:

poet, mystic, lover
claim his glance for their own:
but only the dead who never
lift eye or cry, or name him
shall own him at the end:

since he and they dwell far
above, below mobbing desire,
and indifferent to each other
separate go their way
into no human day.

CREDENTIALS

I would it were possible to state in so
few words my errand in the world: quite simply
forestalling all inquiry, the oak offers his leaves
largehandedly. And in winter his integral magnificent order
decrees, says solemnly who he is
in the great thrusting limbs that are all finally
one: a return, a permanent riverandsea.

So the rose is its own credential, a certain
unattainable effortless form: wearing its heart
visibly, it gives us heart too: bud, fulness and fall.

HERE THE STEM RISES

deflowered forever.

the bird is wise only
in ways of quiet

time is a lithe fruit
bending above us

too old for comfort
too raw for falling

here no slim morning
steps out of the sea

no season of snow
no hear-ye of thunder

no chameleon crawling
of youth or of age

not even a now
nor an I nor a you

how many the folded
hands. O how lovely

the words never spoken

THE WORKMEN

This is the body the seasons sold for money—
one by one they guarded and grew his frame:
we were hardly ready for him and he was ready.
This is the one.

These are the nettles sprung from sweating Cain.
Gather them up: they are holier far than flowers:
let us see the brow of the laborer glisten with them.
These are the thorns.

These are the coldiron embers of Lucifer:
these are the arrogant stars pushed out of heaven.
Then give him a handful of stars: heap stars at his feet.
These are the nails.

This is the prime redwood of all the world.
It is tougher and taller than he: it will swing him high:
it will hold him high forever if so we wish.
This is the cross.

I SING

        the star whose light
my song makes steady,
the face whose look was never
but when my hand had found it,
the word that lovelier stayed
than trees unstressed by season,
what on the earth was seldom
less seldom for my speaking—
pride, delight, deliverance.

This is not greatness, no:
not that consummate gesture
from king whose *fiat fiat*
is blue on distance blue.
His tree-end never dragged
across my coward foothill:
his manacles and thorns
have never clawed or kinged me.

Not these. But few and lonely
the unregarded wait me
to say their *beautiful*
with breath and heart I borrowed:
who but for self I lent
would like me fret and clutter
and be themselves for never.

EXALTAVIT HUMILES

All things despised, capricious, cranky,
have an hour of morning. Sumac jostled
by shouldering oaks to the forest edge—how it burns
clearer than they. And cobweb, no more than an afterthought,
trembles at dawn like new-hammered silver.

The crouching rocks; overlaid
with purest lace.

The wild brown grasses;
a canticle at the furnace door:
Bless the Lord, rime at morning, frost and cold air!

Roots, bound hand and foot, hear and heave mightily,
lie cruciform, await the breaking spell.

For a moment nothing is wasted, nothing of no moment:
to the banquet grace calls, grace clothes the unwanted poor.

I AM RENEWED

to rising by that sun
sets courage like a summer round my roots
and welcomes me to stature.

I am renewed to breathing by that bread
sent like a sunrise to my dark
bringing me someday, morrow.

My blood that walks as sullen as a millstream
trumpets the joining of that wine of His.

My life that folds to burial grows bold
and hobbled in its windings climbs the grave.

My ashen words puff up in flame
infused with four winds of a word *arise*.

My hollow breast takes heart at hearing Him
sing like a star above its broken roof.

My feet clear gardens in the greying snow:
my winters die for mention of His name.

O let these words remind His wounds of me

LIGHTNING STRUCK HERE

If stones can dream, after some hundred years
shouldering weight, making a wall inch onward
heaving it up a hill, braking its roll,
being only half above ground, taking the crack

of frost, the infernal sun, the insinuating, sleepy moss:—
if stones can long to stand up naked, a new creation
a horizon; where the wall goes
what shires, forests, it holds—
                         I suppose the dream
might rise, might arc, take color and stance of these
birches that fan out suddenly, bursting the wall
so when we come on them, all that remains
is a shambles. Lightning struck here
is a first thought. But no: a dream
shook from the mud, the interminable years, and lives.

The Gospel According to Me

1. LONELINESS (Joseph speaks)

To be a part of things, to be apart from them:

Every spring I dunged and pruned the peach row
on south hillside: every autumn, like a stranger
took down the fruit whose face met my surprise
with its odor and wet, only half remembered or deserved.

Or watched from a doorway, artisans
summoning out of a dumb stick some form of beauty,
the fine grain emerging along hand or arm like a pulse,
every sigh of the blade saying, *I did not do that.*

Or parleyed with old trees
that shift painfully in the noon wind, heads together
nodding a memory awake. I did not lead them there:
they were already old when my father slept
a boy's drowsy noon in their shade.

I had even less to do with the stars
that having led her to me, bring her still face to me
evening and dawn, making of evening and dawn
one tranquil ecstasy.
　　　　　　　　Blade, hoe, manhood—
what have my tools to do with What wakes in her?

2. SAID GOD

I would give my Son to them.
In a field of flowers, wide dawn to dusk,
one hesitant flower more, only one more:

in a sky already great with stars,
one star more at the edge, hardly in evening.

He will not make turmoil: one child more
led by his father's hand into a park of children:
one voice adds little: one voice to a choir,
another among the swings, linked in a ring-around.

They take him easily to heart: more is but
merrier: he asks
so little of heart or world. He will never trouble
the country children of men with who am I.

Only to pause intent over their games. Never to say
Children: I am all your bloom and odor and starlight.

3. THE COAT

This is the coat His mother fitted
at hearthlight weeping fondly. In three seasons—
summer was her angel, fall bent her boughs
crone winter mothered her maidenhead—
she stitched Him in and out by the nodding fire:
O heartbeat soft as snow on high snow falling,
vein as the veined grape delicate,
my body's shuttle closes you in white linen.

This is the coat my mother's love went buying
to warm me, naked and shivering one
she heard all night peeking her heart for shelter.
This skin she buttoned to my chin, these eyes
she kissed to light, and gave me over
to the stinging hand of twelvemonth winter.

It wears me well. She in cunning stole me
from the bolt Christ, won my pattern
wheedling and whispering with Mary at a churchdoor.
I am more kin of Him than hers
who cut and seamed me till her body bled.

O see Him live in me, not I:
I put him on and strut my coat-of-pie.

4. IN SUM, LIKE THIS

Who you are
let astounded midnight say
that saw itself flooded with day

or springtime that came around
subtly on the world's wheel
and saw you, small and larger, walking its ground

or suave on a boy's tongue
the air making your words
and taking them grandly, a whole summer of birds:

let that mother tell
whose earth and heaven were small
between hearthside and village well

or the dumb tree that bears
pegged down, posted as ours
forever, the unsearchable human years.

5. THE MEN ON THE HILL

There is still time to escape
the hill where ruin hangs,
the dry, lax throat of doom.

Tall as veiled spears they hem him,
the proud and diehard women.
Their hearts bleed in their eyes,
their eyes run on to death, their wits
in little feeble rivers run the ground.

Mark what holds them still:—
his spastic dying cry:
for murderers no lightning:
a thirst to curse all springs
our tongues are laid against.

There is less than nothing here.
Nothing were yet something
if stones would rise and grate
a syllable of God: if hands were sprung
a moment only from the trap of nails.

But death has staked him off
and bound him for its baggage:
heaving no miracle, the hill
sighs to a long sun westward:

the sky runs red with torches,
the city blinks us blind
and only death is savior.

6. PLAY SAFE; His Friends

Of course death was hard, hard for the poor.
Yet one finally took it in stride,
closing a father's eyes, seeing the mild slumbering
seas turn monstrous.

But this:

God, unutterable,
friend, mildly poured
over days and years. What words were left us
(this hard exchange, this other side of death?)

Whether we turned locks in a remote alley
or pushed off into seas and stars: the dawn
rose to him, evening breathed him.
It was always
never again to be safe, summed up our lives.

7. BELIEVE

That delicate honeycomb Christ took to mouth,
that plundered nest was sweet, to lips grown grey
with Judas kiss and gall. Not since Mary's milk
had earth offered in cup or lip
such words as bees, this way and that shifting
assuring: the dead flower lives: even death serves.

The dismembered fish too,
ikthus for Christ, stared up at the fearful
fishermen. They tossed unseaworthy
when the walker of waves stood there; the floor
pitched them green. When he had eaten away all
but literal arrangement, the skeleton said with its mouth
Jesus Christ, Son of God, Savior.
                              Death again: the eyes
even of a dead fish crying: *believe or drown.*

8. GOOD NEWS IN A BAD TIME

Women who come to mummy you: trees
on that road, stood in commencing flesh
and said with a new tongue

I am risen. A hundred resurrections lined the dawn
but they thought: we will give his ghost cold comfort
and wind him like a Pharaoh in long linen.
They had nothing to offer life. Of what use in that mouth

honeycomb or fish? He must grow his own flesh
a tree from its root.

They stand where he cast the squared stone aside.
They run and run, but the news

is far as the tremendous drowning
world of trees, that drank from his infinite
roots: runs far ahead, far as years
as morning, as this unhurried tree.

9. THE BIG WIND

Their lives rounded in a backcountry brogue
now to see, at crowd's edge, the fine Athenian profiles
agape, scenting their delicate language like
odor of muscatel or honey:

Peter and John, it is Babel crashing about your ears.
The Spirit, impatient of gross and exquisite tongues, of known
and unknown gods, has riven the abominable tower
The undivided tongues

are abroad, are a wildfire.

You; never again constrained
by scarecrow gestures, by hem or haw. You; to see
agonized at the crowd's edge, the faces emptied of guile,
their human wisdom consumed in a stench of straw.

EACH DAY WRITES

in my heart's core
ineradicably, what it is to be man.

Hours and hours, no sun rises, night sits
kenneled in me: or spring, spring's
flowering seizes me in an hour.

I tread my heart amazed: what land,
what skies are these, whose shifting weathers
now shrink my harvest to a stack of bones;
now weigh my life with glory?

Christ, to whose eyes flew,
whose human heart knew, or furious or slow,
the dark wingbeat of time: your presence give
light to my eyeless mind, reason to my heart's rhyme.

THE CASTLE (Heidelberg)

Even the elegant monuments stop their breathing,
buttons and swords dropped, suave features blank.
Now an icecream day, the sun's snapping lens
make mock of gentlemen awry, these leaning towers
whom children and time undo, whose shadows flee them:
at length proved wrong, proved dolts and dispensable.

Then in one place, a flush of roses
rooted in dust, climbs armor and ruined lace
regardless: at looted heart
it blooms and beats, a marvelous revenge.

LITTLE HOURS

I

Mother, at that word your eloquent body spoke
I search another word vainly as Gabriel.
O witnessing your consent, he saw
an axis planted deep in our human soil;
history, fear, defeat, aeons and nations
turned, would turn forever about your village room
declaring like figures in time's rickety tower
the lightning strike, this only and central hour.

Whom the world could not contain is detained in you.

Since Love in entering, so builds your hidden doorway,
consent again, receive me for child I pray:
your nourishment, your silence, your face averted,
your hands serving excellent bread and meat: your heart
apart in its own country, heaven descended
to four low walls and a dim evening fire.

II

Winter is hard: it reminds us how that mother,
heavy and meek at term, set foot on her dolorous road.
Her trees, ample and tender at summer
were slit and groaning beggars the wind went through:
the sun that clothed and companied her angel:
what fierce looks from him, and scant comfort now!

Mother: because the ungracious season did not rise
—at your footfall, for knowledge of whom you carried,—
leap cliffs with roses, melt the tigerlike ice
into tame brooks for you—

                        because north wind blew
and summer hid—enter stilly my heart
whose winter your footfall breaks all apart.

III

Like a waterfall, from what height falling
he came to her; falling, filling her body.
That vessel, brimming with him, O never shall fail.

or entered her like a sun its morning, starting what flowers—
from her footfall and welcome, an inextinguishable day.
that dawn lifting light to us, O never shall darkness own.

or came in echoes of that living anvil
forming him, calling him: be loud in me, love O loud:
until his thunders owned her breast utterly.

he came as tongue to her bells. O from that shaken
and living tower, what music flies: my soul
does magnify who makes my body great.

or came in a tide, riding her pure lands under—
tender, O living rain: he fell to her to rise
in hundredfolds up from her secret garden.

But mostly in need, asking her flesh to clothe him.
O because love ran uncontrollably to that meeting,
from her arms, her breast, He walks into our lives.

II
ENCOUNTERS

II
ENCOUNTERS

EVE

It was for love of me
Adam undid Christ. And I must encounter
of my sour body that golden fruit
Mary; and say to her

how firm we wove and grasped
the ropes that scourged him
what thorns we grew, our first tears'
harvest for his crown.

Woman to woman's heart
I will go. Miles are years from Eden to that hill
but I will take for sign, if so she know me
blood on my face

I will follow
the unhealed scar the tree Christ dragged
opens in time

the poor go
for comfort to the poor.

Across years, across the stilled
hearts of our sons: drawing the vicious
thornbrake aside, sundering the serpentine rope
her hand reaches my own.

ABEL

One blood veined us, stem and fruit
weighing our mother Eve. *Brothers*
said her burning eyes: *see, hand*
must lock in hand: fingers root
in no rock than this other: Abel
in Cain, younger in his brother.

My mother, the worm that raveled Eden
tents in the parent tree.
                              New lambs
sniff and shy at my blood: go red fleece
teach death to my mother.

ABRAHAM

To see my small son
running ahead: pausing above a flower,
bringing some trifle of hedgerow
wearying, sighing, seeking my hand

unable in all his being
to give death credence,
his heart agile
to prove youth upon a ditch or stile:

to see this you must know
my heart like kettledrums commanded
alarms and marches, shook old age
like treason from its majesty.

My heart now
drums
I am nearer I am death

Who is child now? who is old? my tears
or his song? I am sift of dust
in that Hand unmercifully blown

Love Me, His thunder never cried
Love me
my child's eyes never cried
until this dawn
and under
    under
    my knife

SAINT JOSEPH

She walked noon fields
bearing the child in arms.
Trees stood stock still, even in May wind.

Some task of women
bowed her head, set fingers flying,
a busy stillness at the heart.

Like learning and entering
paradise: from labor to mild joy, from action

to adoration.
          At the still center she
and the child aimlessly gathering
wild grasses: into one hand, the scattered leaves gathering
of the universe.

CHRIST

Words are outer form
wherein majesty might near,
                         if it so please:
of limb and mien not substance,
but light; glancing,
                         announcing: lo, he cometh.

Words summon her too,
                         the mother infolding
like a kerchief, odor and form
                         of him who lay there:
so in repose her body grew
a spiritual space to round
                         and radiate you:

friends, whose memory
calls up your ghost at cockcrow:
                         there and not there

if tears glister or no:

so, struck from your holy flesh,
                         distance and
access, our words begin
                         like lepers' bells: O come
not near.

ATLAS

A fern at window
eyes
    the great-boned maple steadying for death. Cat

sat at a bullfight, and was bored.

Samson's falling
takes time
down with him:

greatness wears its lionheart and fleece.
He will never say it (say it!)
Good bye, manifestoes of summer love.

                                     Atlas

take up the cross.

SAINT JOHN BAPTIST

I

When first I heard his voice, I wakened
drowning in my mother.

She stooped and touched my eyes.
Womb, desert, dungeon, light and dark.

Then. A sword forbade me to grow old; it cut
time like a parasite from eternity.

Could death have eyed and pierced my body, could I
have stood upon the nails an hour,
would he take warning from his murdered shade
casting his fate in smoky runes
with points of light
like lips where death had fastened?

I follow from sad limbo
till death unfasten, till his rising
unwind and wear me
aureole   choir   crown

SAINT JOHN BAPTIST
II

In the mirror a sword made
descending
briefer than image a stream carries
beyond,
I saw John old: eyes cold, hair silver.

Look how I save you
sang the blade strongly:
dwarfing honors, prophecies by rote
a stalemate heart; freedman, stand free.

                I caught in two hands
this unripe storm-shaken fruit, by hate
(by love) tossed down
tasted at soul's root that wine's stream.

SAINT ANN
(who bore a daughter in late life)

Hand that folded and laid aside my fabric
as it pleased Him
         when it pleased Him, shook me out,
billowed and filled me like a silken tent
         A voice, He comes
shaking the women up
         at dawn, barefoot
through burning snow, and shouting *manna manna*

APOSTLES

Ringed Him about then,
not twelve profiles for a frieze.
Caesars, prophets, judges: would history have tossed
a rust coin on our future? doubt it.

No Moby, no conquistadors
but landmen groaning green on a two-mile pond
and He dry-shod as a Red-Sea Jew
cradling
distempered night to a babe's closed eye.

we grew gentle to harbor
Christ's dream of us
someday. Beached, and found
twelve dead men flung, wearing our faces drowned.

LAZARUS

Sister, you placed my heart in its stone room
where no flowers curiously come, and sun's voice
rebuffed, hangs on the stones dumb. What I could not bear
I still must hear. Why do your tears fall?

why does their falling move Him, the friend, the
unsuspected lightning: that He walk our garden
with no flowers upon His friend?

what did He say in tears (grief
scalding my hands, cold hands springing
sleep like a manacle) drawing my eyes a space
that had seen God, back to His human face?

SAINT PETER

A cock mounted the tall
rock where His body bled. I choose
that rock to stand: man
and clean of hand and blessed, whose
even second choice was Christ.

THIRST

In him no beauty was
but body racked and robbed
and blood predicting darkly
no comeliness   no wonder

seven seas came marching
winds ran through his caved
breast   the sun was armored

womb on womb
unborn interminably
I started in his longing
and puffed his tongue to drought

in him no beauty was
no comeliness   no wonder

who yet when he was lifted
had drawn all things to him

a fist to his face came sorrow
a thirst   the thought of me

SAINT STEPHEN

That day stones fell
I stood and died
unknowable, a mound of dust for heaven
to make man of.
               That day stones beat
like stone beasts for a forced entry
to eat my heart: I prayed awhile
then opened brief and tossed them meat.
They ate and died of it: unproofed against
my living phial, great love.
               That day
stones flew like hail of stones at first:
my dolorous flesh took their brute will
but stones transformed
to tongues, whispered at every wound:
welcome.
        That day stones flowered
to dark rose-field Christ walked and gathered.

SNOWMAN

The children wrapped up and skeined out and
rolled downhill death, who is ludicrous

but king too, from coal eyes surveying
from ruined mouth saying: *it is all like me:*

no blue or red of vein or heart
fired and set afoot, I do permit me.

The dwarf at shoulder, peering out of eyes
secret and simian, I do dispense with.

But head to boot one element, one temperate
cold requiring.
                        His fallen coals weep and are granted:
spare me sight of the unlike world, its hearts and

heats and blueveined men

HEAR EVER SO GENTLY

Permanent beauty stands
nowhere under the tense
mainspring of time.

while I praise
color and voice of flowers
stealing my heart aside

so frail they are, this night's
starlit air has felled them.

cathedral takes
enemy year after year
deeper the spiritual thrust
on stained and wrinkled stone.

somewhere between its bones'
imperceptible wound
and the star-crossed flower

above a rust of bloom
under the doomed tower
hear: ever so gently

a main and springing hour

TREE: OCTOBER

under that summer cloud
whose rain is red and gold

around that vase's cunning
figures whom storm and calm
scatter to make again

about that summering swan
whose plumage winter hastens
away
      beneath those bells
whose beat broods on the air:

music, plumage, rain
whatever image hung

the great tree at heart

is fled   is flown   is spent.
skeleton: element

MEN WERE THE IMAGE

Unlike a fish
that gestures feebly
with waving fronds from far back in time
I am still unborn
         or a bat, blind
Icarus aground, limping in harness along:

trees confound death
by uprightness: they answer violence like a
gospel man:
        when storm made evident its brute will
and we, not falling to knee, rued dearly

men were the image: in calm a dance gesture,
in sorrow, joy. We shook night from limb
and stood: an arched instrument loud with them.

MORE LIKE THE SEA

(A man is more than two sticks crossed.
He is more like the sea, bringing up God knows what
at any moment: Conrad.)

Nail him to sticks
he stands free, makes sense
of agony, of sticks and stones.
No grafting him on: his fruits
are free, and other: more men loved,
more year's intensities. He ranges, rejoices
the horizon sorrow lifts him to.

Look how hands refuse
all but gift. That blood will flow
red red against bitter
hemlock, maple sweet. Blood writes
what heart provides: God knows what
that sea brings up.

God bring that sea safe
—safe is no word for him—but a
surf home, shuddering its coast
crying hoarse in its falling
victory.

CHILD ABOVE A FLOWER

                 unsure
if he regards
or is regarded.
           Both is a truth
older will fade.
Come, said flower
race me to evening.
             Time is a way
no one knows.
          Who
goes there?
           who went there
answer man's tears, sighs

flower's ghost. Growth is a death
on my youth laid.

AN OLD WOMAN IN DEATH

For words words;
                  death's instantaneous
waterfall
granted all at once
what sun fumbles weeks upon,
                       and only debatedly
brings to pass: I say spring

that springs her absent eyes:
like flowers whose seed dies in
temperate air, they fade here: but in height
elsewhere, are majestic blue

blue wept her eyes when she cried aloud:
in fear or exaltation, no man knows.
The woman who died
shook a worn garment aside

bride somewhere again
                    by loving
                         makes beautiful.

WHICH WAY IS MAN?

Hemlocks in row, heads bowed beneath snowfall
like abstract old men, raven of hair once

but age is upon them: sorrow and reversal
in one night's course,
                          gently exhorted
into longsufferance by winter birds: in moonrise,
twilight, inching their shadow onward.
                                         Eternity
is eventual: the trail sparse and
wavering: a star's flare, a wounded bird in snow:

vocation a ghost's cry: *which way is man?*

WE LOVE

about trees: past is never tall enough,
future too tall. Another spring will tell.

Tell another spring
                    I will be there, and fairer.
I become myself
that throat of swan
that striding giant I decree myself.

We love: in trees or men, how many die
forward on the blade.
                    I see men like forests
striding, like swans riding, always
royally: though lowly afoot, striding into death.

What we love: there are not blades enough.

GO DOWN ON KNEE

I saw an old wife stricken, the man
bending painfully above: *let me serve, be
eyes, limbs.*
            Man, wife, wearing for better for
worse, the other's flesh, rent and patch: *I do.*
Bridal gown is yellow as bone, raveled

like youth out many a gay and slower
mile: stained bowler and waistcoat, a
rusty charmer.
            Yet all days since, I see
visible things of this world, faultless
and heartening, go down on knee before, fashion
music toward, measure hope and
decline upon
            the least audible heartbeat
of this holy darkness: *I love you.*

A STATUE OF THE BLESSED VIRGIN, CARVED IN WOOD

Wood is noble when it forgets resemblance

and like the first idea of tree
stands straight up and awaits creation.

Then art is arbitrary; it decrees

what moment Mary will pause in. Forbidding
lips their sound, shapes a phrase
of universal mercy. And the delicate outthrust foot
protests and starts: you are my errand.

LOVE IS A DIFFERENCE

Water is the shaping form whose blade
cuts
  fish to jeweled finish.
Man? out of native air
soon lost.

But lends reason to,
whispers *here and now* to
      air cut to his profile:

as a bell lifts
    to pour on 4
winds their christening:
      or majestic birds,
         daring
a perilous clearing,
    teach light its spectrum.

RADICAL STRENGTH

                    issues in marvels:

crucial delicate finger at flute stop.

Hill easing itself like tiger's body,
                              around one
blind tuft of violets.

A spring after, felled oak, one
heartbeat unspent: one
handful of leaves
                    in a dead hand.

BEETHOVEN'S VIOLIN

(*for Carol and Jerry*)

Birnam Wood across the plain, marches
season after season, into itself.
                    But the first day of all
dawns from that throat.

Tenderness and strength
do not dwell in one life.
                    Yet the violin
summons tears and commands action.
Its best face is a smile;
             it is achieved, sings

fearfully and wonderfully made, sings
the violin. I have taken wings at morning
I have searched the uttermost sea: there is no one
to love me like this lover.
                  I am Eve, sings the violin:
I am taken from his side:
                  I heal with my body,
with sounds his hands make
the wound
I
opened
him.

III

THE WORLD
FOR WEDDING RING

SAINT JOSEPH SPEAKS

(*in memoriam: Ed Willock*)

I am near to you
and yet not near
biblical man recedes.
A great page is not Joseph. Edify, glorify?

I send the morning
red, newborn, up—and make of yes and no,
of God and you, one impregnated hour,
parts of one heart, its red and readiness.

TWO DAYS AFTER DEATH

Too soon for poems;
I write in clumsy grief
Mary's unlettered face

never
to flourish like bay tree, be our ornament
light the winter scape, our kings' incense
our fiery child on January night

never. I walk past
trees plunged upright,
an iron world. Breathe
like swords, the zero air of loss.

KINDER TIMES?

        But what use were angels
in the raw world? Christ's hands and heart
time hammered open.
              He pours
human over us. Breathe deep, question his wounds
what way now?

Listen; the chime, the synonym
made death a wine, turned all His body rose.

HE PAUSED AMONG MEN

    and spoke: *coopers, craftsmen, shepherds*
blessed is the prophet
whose blood speaks in his stead. Search death out

and sought death in their cities, and was taken
young years and all, composed in ground
like wintering bees

and after respite stood again
in tremendous mime, (shut doors sprung,
permeable world)
all man would come to.

DEATH CASTS NO LIGHT ON THE MIND

It is not for that; not
permeable at all, an Easter cross.

He crossed himself, and climbed.

Then   then

imagination springs; it tastes
mulberries, risen tigers, Himalayas,
summer lightning—

He leaped eternity
(whisper goes),
                     a tiger to its prey.

BLIND MAN

Dawns that stand like chevaliers to man
and open tranquilly and in turn

stood, wooden in me: eyes, two
driven pegs: not eyes

clear blue or grey—but whittled, a marionette's

or mole's. *Day* my mother whispered. Her fingers
sought like a healer's mine; *day*, but no dawn.

Words, hearts, noon light, Lucifer,
love perhaps—all wear my eyes'
eyeless skin.
    And that seer
       shivering in deathsweat
does he have tears to spend
on his hands' botch—no eyes, no tears
for even him?

SAINT MATTHEW, PUBLICAN

Caesar's coin
tastes no death. Turning full face
it lies full in face. *No god but Caesar*
says the gold eye that lights, like hell
nothing to buy.

Follow Me. Superscription, face
are sallow rust, a ruin
graves, armies, ignorant time
conspire toward. Caesar weeps at last
is man at last, long lives.

HOPE

All night the fretful cricket

skirrs like a conscience, night in his bones
light in his points of eye—hope

illiterate and fey,
a cock raising minuscule dawn

match flare might make, or candle end
and he foolish cry *dawn!* at the false dawn

that wakened him for death.

How small a thing is hope—
hairspring body, mind's eye, and all endangered.

EVENTS

Events are orthodoxy, he would say,
submitting like any son.
The way a fruit tastes of itself
he tasted sacrifice.
No thirst but for that cup
engendering thirst.

Credo is event, would say
to a brother's face
by birth or death brought near—
a descending god he saw, a god
sprung from his tears.
Piety of experience
bound him in web.
He wore the world for wedding band.

Here
A few notes toward a life.
Words, words are what we buried.

Look; time wears new features, time takes heart.

MOON

Battlements, tombs—no longer
populous or loud, the living
towns go underground.
The impalpable dead are come.
All Souls' cock on the steeple
summons them out of doors
to touch autumnal hands
to breathe the estranging air.
Toward false dawn they renounce
abulia and death;
passionate, bodied, cry;
whey-faced people of light
cannot abide. But black
is beautiful at last.
Dark, dark be the spell. Public
man never made love.
Grow him a dark grove.

THE POEM WAITS ON EXPERIENCE

    a ghost in offstage darkness; no lines,
no wig, no eyes. I have not loved the poor,
I have not died yet.

Yet I am poor
as all the shanties of the world
gone up in flares;
on a rotted springs
a junky's baked skeleton.

Here, for its worth, the poem.

THE POET AS OBSERVER

I sit like a dunce in the incandescent noon
stool, cap, notes

a liberated blind man
whose eyes bear him like wings
out of night's stinking nest, into this world.

Intellectual vision, reality by definition?
No. The Jesuit mind, a Homer

assembles fleets, sails for its continent
across seas tamed by the ordering governing glance.

But to light on and finger the world, bit by bit
an old woman in the flea market—

junk, onions, ordure. Ingredients and parts.
The old fingers, wise as eyes, come on something. A yes.

TO WALLACE STEVENS

In each of us you live on, the lodged seed
of empiric imagination
from a great pod blown on death's virile wind.

Credo, we said, *credo,* mirror
to mirror, an inhumanity
before no god.

You are our puzzle. You, naked as we
amid the poverties of our world
—flowers, donkeys, angels meek as water—
cunningly
surpassed us in an hour. Refusing our credo
your marvelous method
made dawn, made a world, made marriage of light and flesh

without God, you said. But is decree of absence
final, when the imagination yields
like a god's brow
godlike men, armed, passionate for their world?

1961

I summon my parents, a jubilee morning.
When in gold vestments I came down
to kiss them where they stood, their tears and mine

were a clear pressing of the eighty-year vine.
I touched their faces, a gentle unweathered grain
the blind might visualize, as of green leaves
up from exposed ground.
                    What winter fury
that moment tempered, they and I know.

IN MEMORIAM (I)

Seldom, death's virulent fires fail
—disease, consuming effort of mind—
all or any, each an end.

No, but for once
clarify in act
detente, defeat.

One harrowing profitless winter,
sun turned a blank page.
The world arose, illustration
of its own blackened magnificent form.

HOMILY

Said; a cleric worth his salt
will salt his bread with tears, sometimes.
will break bread
which is the world's flesh, with the world's poor,
count this his privilege and more—

And called Saint Paul for exemplar
whose fingers stitched the church a robe,
its crude device
a Christ crucified, wrought of his workman's hands
which the foul dust had sealed
utter and unforeseen, priest and lord.

No disdain must stain the workman's hands
that such task own.
It is all one, I cried. The Lord
upbears the poor man's hand in His, His fruit.
Gospel has it so; one, grape, tendril, shoot and root.

The confession of humanity is our honor, clerics.
Celibate, father—that irony
time urges to term—

You are the poor man's food.
Or great Burgundy, rotting, sours time's ground.

GOOD CAIPHAS

   perfumes, resin, nard—
they fell in showers
on fallen Christ.
We will make sandalwood of him
and store like bees
honey in his stern eyes.
Someone, ages gone
will touch a spring
and chant the open-sesame
and find our golden Pharaoh safe as wheat.

Or so they thought.
But blood, blood
writes red
one name; when dawn breaks
it wakens, and we cry—
is this the wasted vine
God's hand has healed, pressed, poured?

Flesh too from one dark loom
is ours and his, whole cloth.
When winds take him on high
we follow too.
That watchful hurrying prince's eye
sails us to the Father.

THE FACE OF CHRIST

The tragic beauty of the face of Christ
shines in the face of man;

the abandoned old live on
in shabby rooms, far from comfort.
Outside,
din and purpose, the world, a fiery animal
reined in by youth. Within
a pallid tiring heart
shuffles about its dwelling.

Nothing, so little, comes of life's promise.
Of broken men, despised minds
what does one make—
a roadside show, a graveyard of the heart?

Christ, fowler of street and hedgerow
cripples, the distempered old
—eyes blind as woodknots,
tongues tight as immigrants'—all
taken in His gospel net,
the hue and cry of existence.

Heaven, of such imperfection,
wary, ravaged, wild?

Yes. Compel them in.

IRONIES

What moves me are ironies
that draw the mind free of habitual
animal ease. Sough of tides in the heart,
massive and moony, is not our sound.

But hope and despair together
bring tears to face, are a human ground;
death mask and comic, such speech
as hero and common man devise, makes sense

contrive our face. To expunge
either, is to cast snares for the
ghost a glancing heart makes
along a ground, and airy goes its way.

NOT YET

I remember this;
hands of Christ laid
across man's brow and eyes.
The man of action stilled,
a single vein
named thought, named love
reaming him through.

Christ and Mary know me
true grain and crooked, one.
She turning eyes from Him, as Beatrice once
bestows infrequently
a glance brimming with Christ.
And flaming souls tongue
mother and son draw near!

but here
            purgation and afar

TERESA OF AVILA

Almighty God could make again
did malice unmake the world
from my turning heart, a world of use enough.

When I ride under moon, it is
in love   *in love* frosty wheels sing.

Profiles, trades, brogues, oxen
milk-white, hillsides
holding, still as old shepherds, valleys of lambs—

a universe His majesty had not
foreseen? seed, pollen, world
by what gravity drawn, by wind driven,
nest in this dun body,
burr to my heart.

LANDSCAPES THERE ARE

    of formal will and silken atmosphere;
where is the legendary Chinese brush
drawing man
             gently into stillness?

Not conquest of height
nor grandiose will
but an uncopyable phrase

a bough in one direction
running.
        Like a child's legend or man's death
or *I love you,* never in history repeating itself.

THE LENS

Poignant, this counterpoint—
young lives unwrung by the world:
fretful poplars, enduring the season's
gradual death blow,
exposed root and musculature
huddling for last stand.

Time grinds so hard and clear—
your lens, young John and Margaret.

But who sees youth
                        going?
                                    it is here
or never.
            I cannot, for all of love
bind in one healing image
the scabrous limbs of trees
and the supple hands,
                        eyed and sensuous
that break and stack old bones
a hecatomb, a night picnic fire.

THE EFFORT OF UNDERSTANDING

Look up.
To claim the air as that hawk does—
fatuous image.
At such height, earth is a poor
glomerate of no smells, no elbows.

                                 I had rather

here.

                    But there
catch breath, sometimes;

what does he, what would I, know?

A STATUE OF THE BLESSED VIRGIN, CARVED IN IVORY

Such a curve time grew;
at viable tip of inauspicious starts
is you.
      The race strives to bear,
                            a Swedish
fountain-piece,
              sons and daughters
upward,
        like waters,
                in hope of you.

THE LEVITE

(a ninth-century crucified, Metropolitan Museum)

A thousand-year-old corpse has no redress;
undistracted, head upon breast

In that confessional guise, all is his grist

whose blood is rust, whose body
clings like a locust shell its tree.

We read the image. One Friday
one hour, signatory

of guilt and guilt expunged; we
roundelay about this pole

airing an argument which unopposed
we win, you lose.

Simply, though under wormwood
under old nails and joists, under

a stroke of ancient style that isolates
(time's genius) your visionary gift—

compounded, a calculus of time—

yet, we beseech, have done
let the pierced arms have done

stretched loins, drained heart, all
their tragic charade. The dead may come

their task done, into resurrection—
an hour, a transcendent hush

a stranger's face at door, a voice,
unfaltering hands, our evening bread.

AWAKENING

When I grew appalled by love
and stood, a sick man
on feeble knees
peering at walls and weather
the strange outdoors, the house of strangers—
there, there was a beginning.

The world peeled away
usual upon usual
like foil in a fire.
Fell that day, all summer
That day, mind made an elegy
world might gape and weep.

I forget it now.
But remember too; a green tree
all winter's ignorant winds trampled in vain.

HAVING ENDURED THE DEAD
(*for Tony Walsh*)

    who without hands trouble the latch
who without sight
darken the world's fraudulent show

having endured the dead

who without tongue moil the night's lust
laugh it to black scorn

having endured the dead.

Last night Russ Whalen's death
struck us in face, his friends.

You bore it hardest, who dwell for years
on rotting Young Street. *Poor man*
the poor name you; they forgive
Christ for your sake.

Behind a crooked shutter
death's blear look
takes your measure too, waiting day out.

SAINT PETER SPEAKS

Neither prideful nor superhuman—
a racked man
a haunted man, better;
far from false heart
and big promissory words.

Hands articulate
in stillness or action;

another face among faces
in twilight; out of whose body
emanations, uses of work and love
streamed like night mist
up from earth. A racked man,
a haunted man, I knew him.
If God put on a country face,
hefted man's gear, wrung
like any son, sustenance from his acre—

all were in this image,
intent, hereditary, skillful
an unmistaking wit

Mazed by courtesies
multiplied in secret,
I had forgotten
the numbed bewilderment
that stole our wits
at the violent end.

But think now to recover
semblance of order
from that willful disordered murder.
I remember Tiberias sea
storming straight up
at the wind's trump.

On that green hell one face appears
sunken, nearing its peace, then clearer.

He walked the storm. He made peace be.
He summoned me, as though sea
were road and rest, Himself.
Racked man, haunted man—
the saving pain of life
is to drown out of one's human
stinking corpse,
a taken foolish fish
at wit's end drawn into being.

DEATHBED

Failure of action was that hour's loss.
Mind had its empyrean
fastidious, cleaner than bone
he came and went, our doors and minds assaulting

with lordly assumption; *you may
if it please you, stand idle as park statues
casting cold tears
on dogs or the rotting poor. Not I.*

And so resigned the world. For what world
what hands contrived, by what means fending—

Like dogs or the poor, he said.

Failure of heart, they said.

GRANDFATHER POEM

What men desire
passionately
or in rumination
he let go

today, tomorrow
a chance hook for an odd thing,

closing his eyes
as sun goes
a thousand times
then once
for all, named death.

Semblance, then evidence—
see in old eyes
lucid now
a night
no enterprise
no cloud may stain.

MY MOTHER

I know love's
are large claims, but hers
modest
as hands;
a word, a flower,
a child's face for instrument.

Even in dreams, hands speak
Speak?
Creation is summons.
Their speech creates
awakenings.

THE HOLY INNOCENTS

Dying held no dismay.
in our mother's arms, so brief
Full was her breast, sword ran too.
It might have been play; red and white
the fountain leapt—*drink,* then

whether in foul places we lay briefly
or fleeing the fowler we sped here,
thanks to Christ whose love translated us.

Staying to learn we are but men, were word
too dull for joy at a descending sword.

NOW ALL TOGETHER ON THE ONE TWO

Contain me!
stag's nostril and eye
led like a smoke
through shape and shape.

A rampageous tree, for lightning space
struck hoof to earth, and
sped was, or was tree

A friend's eye
his beat of heart
first to last stroke—
endearing youth's shape,
enduring age
weathered hope.

PARABLE

Cripples died at pool side,
in roadways, ditches, porches.
No help for it.

And if by crutch or crook one stood—
a most unsettling genius;

delays, deferring eyes;
superior vision

declined. No miracle.

No *why*. Death kept a close mouth.

LAZARUS

I

Silence rolled over, over my body its
monstrous milling; a fine dust
settled on millstone death.

If truth were told, the white dust could not tell it
even when that young Magian
cried *open-sesame* and puffed me to a man.

LAZARUS
II

After my world was only
two women above me, and they murmuring
gradual farewell, like bells or heartbeat—

I could not care, nor summon
to whisper *I do not care*. Yet for them
heart stood like a stricken drummer: one beat more.

It was not death!
Though his steps slower fell than the great stone,
he cried; *I am the way*

and banished death away
chiding
from the stone doorway
away
their tears.

TREE (I)

Heart's dulled edge, mind's lessening arc
calamitous old age
unexplainably sweetened!

A dusty hedgerow bird
clings there, blazes
a beggared savior.

IV

NO ONE WALKS WATERS

HOLY WEEK, 1965
(*North Vietnam: the air raids go on*)

For us to make a choice
was always a wrong choice—
why not die in the world
one was born into? what was wrong?

They were patient almost as time.
Their words ate like a tooth.

They looked into our eyes
wild by starts, like the times.
They saw
and marveled, and shook. We saw
out of the edge of the eye
hell;
    out of the center eye
a command. And blinked
their asperges away; *be blind.*

THE WRITING OF A POEM

Greatness of art
is a newborn look, a cry

or the gaze
the dying summon toward the newborn
held before clouding eyes,
a flagon, the unpoured cup of going.

Too sorrowful? say then
greatness is exclusions,
(totems, weights, measures,
woodbins, diets,
midnight arrogance of clocks,
the cat's somnolent metaphysic—

see with a spot I damn them.)

The greatness of art; it cries *reality!*
like a mordant blinded god.

KEEP THE HOUR

I set this down toward May midnight.
A blind moon in search of intellect
walks the waste sky in vain. But listen—

the wild kildeer, deprived, importunate
cries out: *man, man is my passion.*

Enough, all said—
the mind's life, an ironic victory
in a stark hour.

YOU FINISH IT: I CAN'T

The world is somewhere visibly round,
perfectly lighted, firm, free in space,

but why men die like kings or
sick animals, why tears stand
in living faces, why one forgets

the color of the eyes of the dead—

HENRY MOORE IN THE GARDEN

The wrought face
of time and human life
yields to no insolvent poking eye
but is shaped, like infants,
by act and season of love—

I came on your stolen wisdom, Henry Moore,
from a deaf mute
stretched on the earth like Zeus or Christ,
corpse, claimant, porter to hell
couchant on the earth's shield.
When I took his head in my hands
it cracked like an egg, man's touchstone.
The bones shuddered and stilled. He had been lodging
patient as Job's diary
ravens, ambergris, wandering Jews, the deluge.
He spat out Buddha's tooth.

Question that mouth? shout at those ears?
They are not fountain spouts.
They are typography. Period.

The egg of the universe
bakes here.

WE ARE IN LOVE,
THE CELIBATES GRAVELY SAY

They hold Christ up
like twelve earnest athletes at a trampoline, but

if I go, I return He says
skilled in gravity

His continuing declension
like dew or fiery napalm

or the seeding of streams with trout eggs.
The twelve earnest orantes hold their hands

safe as stone up to the absent One
which He presently strikes, forces and fills—

world, and world's beauty.

THE QUESTION

If the world's temperate zone,
then too
its cruel weather,
punishing torrid, arctic.

If freedom, then two wills
conflicting; wild Cain,
smooth-phrased Abel, too good
for foul actual life.

If shelter and shepherd,
then the wild verge of the heart,
extravagance, violence; the lamb
murdered; rot and stench.

If the way,
then no way at all; way lost
last chance, a Potter's waste.

If fiery vine, then sour lees at heart.

If silence, forbearance
under all malice—

O when
when will You have done
imagining men?

MIRACLES

Were I God almighty, I would ordain,
rain fall lightly where old men trod,
no death in childbirth, neither infant nor mother,
ditches firm fenced against the errant blind,
aircraft come to ground like any feather.

No mischance, malice, knives,
tears dried. Would resolve all
flaw and blockage of mind
that makes men mad, sets lives awry.

So I pray, under
the sign of the world's murder, the ruined son;
why are you silent?
feverish as lions
hear men in the world,
caged, devoid of hope.

Still, some redress and healing.
The hand of an old woman
turns gospel page;
it flares up gently, the sudden tears of Christ.

AIR TRIP TO BOSTON

1.

I may become
sharp tongued, intolerant, a sore old man.
It looks as though, sometimes.
Still, have stolen from Rouault's art
the old king's fragile unkillable flower.

Heal-all, sweeten my mind's stream.

2.

Turning a page
I came on your death, Connolly,
the fierce crawl of time
a dragged limb or cross.
Then, your hollowed brows
five, ten years before—
no eyes or face, no particulars.

Rain wash, wind wash, wash of time!
The brow, a bowl
ground perfect on the earth's wheel

for holding of—what? You, empty, know.

3.

The long line of birches—
landing among them at the airstrip edge,
Russian bells or Saint Elmo's fire
or the plumage of swans;
                              one voice
flooding the senses
making truth of the world; *start with us!*

A PITTSBURGH BEGGAR REMINDS ME OF THE DEAD OF HIROSHIMA

Seeing the beggar's sign
lettered and hung like a sandwich board—
"I am blind, suffer from angina
and claim no pension or support of any kind."
the crowd dug deep, the tin can
sang like a wishing well.

These days, everyone being at war,
not to pay dear is to prod the inner horror
awake; speech starting up by heart,
lights going on and off, a Greek sky
where five stars make a god; a voice
we got them there; or *he stood like a bastard here, but*
we took him piece by piece;
shipped his skull home, polished like a gouty
whole head—

Perhaps the poem is odd man out
wherein my foulness
drags forward, touches His flesh
an emperor's birthmark
under beggardry, leprosy.
I am too unschooled to know,
befouled and blinded by the hot droppings
that struck my eyes in sleep, from the great bird
the descending fecal horror.
I stood and shook like ague
—Hiroshima, Nagasaki—
the ungentle names of my memory's youth,
the blue remembered hills
tipping like hell's buckets all their
hot afterbirth on me.

Healer, you would need
stout heart where I must stand;

no bones, nothing to start with
for repair and solace
of the vast meridian horror.
You would peer and poke
a blind man on a dump
tracing—another stone in a
dismembered wall—the Neanderthal
boy's bones, half discernible
in turned-up garden litter,
the obliterated dead, the slight
rhythms of marble tracery or flesh—which?

I believe in the Father almighty
and in Jesus Christ
his risen flesh, indistinguishable
from the permeating stench
that rises, spreads, drifts
on prevailing island winds
when a people goes up, a
mockup of city
slapped together for a brief
sequence—*lights, drone, target*—

Flesh of Christ—
indistinguishable, compounded
yeast, seed, flowering
of flesh of man—
your healing starts here
with the tears the dead
were given no time for, the living
numbed, no heart for.

You, Lazarus, who died and stank—
stagger like a zombie
out of the rubble, jaws
like a burnt carp, unfit for
speech or kiss, that fed
three days down, on carrion death.

Be first. Arise.
Teach the dead their discipline
—shank, hair, ear, articulation—
that rode like furies the inner seas
or fell
a dew on fleece, or settled
like sandman's gifts
on the eyes of sleeping children.

I toss a coin in the wishing flesh
of beggars; coins in the eyes
of murdered children, for buying of
no tears; a coin
in the carp's mouth for Peter's cast.

The dead too; my coin stand you in stead
who went improvident,
no staff or shift, into time's mountain
as though all
were wide door; this momentary hell
a heaven, and passing fair.

THE LEPER

In the torrid breathless noon
birds fall like living embers,
their pirate's eye
seizing on some scrap of offal—

they rise straight up with a rat's scream.
The sun hangs suspended, a sword,
a sentence.

Nuns come and go, among the passive sick.
But a leper crouches, face to ground, in the red dust.
He waits.
Waits? the word fails. An alert dignity and repose;
a lover's or warrior's limbs.

But the hands?

A botch. Arms
end in crude knobs, as though hands
thrust in a vandal's fire, had burnt back to wrists.

Clad in its white clout
the body, a tree
stressed by high wind
(so in its form we see
tempering skill and passion, all at one)

Bow, warrior, manhood,
I mourn him. The foul dust stains him
like a slave's stigma. His body falls
(I see it, a year, two years)
a rotten bow,
a bone the dogs own. The clout falls away
the staved body rolls on, its beauty mauled
in time's swollen Styx.

And you redressing Christ, you easter man
I have no more joy
than a wooden hand scrawls in carrion dust,
a dead eye composes
            in the primary world.

THE ACT OF LOVE

In that hour
body in all its being,
by rare touch of hands and more,
arises healed—

body is one, is more
laid upon
by the loved other.
Blood and flesh a seer
need whisper; *no more; be,*
and be in me.

But epiphany
is brief as lightning flash;
flesh, stricken, falls like ripe yolk
apart. Heart, blind again, beats
like hands the thorn.
Dark, dark the world.

Hopeless, lost,
all excellence and indwelling?
love solved, resolved?

No; they have cast in air
roses, burning thoughts embodied,
a winter or summer child
budding there, flowering;
bird, rainbow; *myself, you.*

CLUNY MUSEUM

The woman's hands weave
shroud or birth clout in air;
a homely face, a woman
not of any countryside I have seen;
a servant perhaps, bowed
with night or dawn labors. And now this death—
hearthstone cold, the beloved son
the single and perfect fruit, crushed under heel.

But a tragic woman stands firm for others' sake.
There is crowding of life on her,
even the dead give place. She stands so.

The living son stands too, as this
wooden man stuck through
with a single murderous spike, cannot know. Come,
I touch his wood. A wildfire; Rise,
the Lord is risen.

MYTHOLOGIES

The word descends
a swan upon flesh;
first gift.

The second,
a girl borne off
by a supernal bull,
the poem gotten.

The third? I cannot know
until all heaven's bells
nod in accord
and pitch me into time.

Meantime, the world;
damnation, rot, renewal,

the unexpected
flesh of man.

IMAGINE, A BOOK CAN BE ALL THIS

A doorway to seasons;
firm ground for walking, air for sight,
a burning landscape. Have only joy there.

A field of flowers—their immortal other.
A crucifix—lector; winter—forbearance;
illness—a transfigured impassioned face

vindicates long sufferance.
Open the book. Wisdom
opens mouth, against all

suppression of death. He is life's
breathing exegete.
Take him, I would, at word.

DARKNESS

I had purposed
a poem; darkness, love's country

but tempestuous night fell
Hell's ink, pitch, ravens, olive gardens,
climacteric of anguish; my argument now.

Tears too, when man
lies dumb, death and life
contending. The ghostly

ungovernable vessel slides in dream;
no, no containing
that tide, that dark voyage.

O I have questions
for the eyeless Bonze that dwells—

why on death's verge, drink the dark,
why on shore, strike cold fire?

Look; across seven seas
morning's miraculous body.

CATECHUMEN

Prophetic soul
stand before history
a blind visionary harper
improvising
time's freedom and sweetness. And lo

imagination speaks—
I christen thee
servitor, emperor.

No. You baptize us
gasping in the world's net,
fish out of element; our milk eye,
our dream, to drift sidewise
in deaf waters; blind,
safe as stone.
Fisher, savior, save from that.

COME AND SEE

Snowmen, birds, the eyed leaves of trees
regard us, the limping dog
on all fours in the gutter after food.

Nothing blind. The mole sees
hard clay is his crystal.

Nothing blind; roots sapient
nerved, eyed, clairvoyant;
a witch stirs a brew I dare you

drink and not change fearfully
in wind and limb and eye,
a mountebank, a baited bear in your

sweet skin. Or a snowman
one black baleful clinker
malevolent upon creator.

A tree
drinks sun, concocts dark
as it took whim. But must see

onset of sawyers, frost, rot—
see
crude fall of that empery.

FOUNTAINHEAD

The open well
collects leaves, waste, vanities;

then, under hands
water runs free again
tideless, endlessly yielding

a cold spring
blessed by wayfaring gods

Immortal hands hold the world in cleft
where waters are born;
lucid, living, a murmurous child.

COMPASSION

I sing bronze statuary
enduring rain and cold,
alert eyes casting back
the sun's burning shafts
a fisher's net soaring,
snare
to catch worlds in.

But in November rain
—rotting asters, scum of leaf—
came on a dying man.

His eyes pled
like an animal at the block
Come to this? And I
kneel upon squalid ground
man's defeat striking
marrow and heart;
Unless I suffer this, you
gentlest Abel, strike
with a glance, Cain down.

THE INMOST MEANING OF CERTAIN SACRED AND NEGLECTED WORDS

Let there be man is one thing—but
let there be this, my hangman? Yes,
no turning aside of nails. I
appoint you to my flesh.

The hard fast rule, cried nails in Him, *is love.*
Climb me, taste me, cried the tree.
I am heavy, crown to limb
with harvest Him.

MAKING SOMETHING

The blind man
longed passionately to see
but wish was vain
while dawn delayed
a false savior, no sight
from his miraculous store.

The cripple dreamed
dancers and tumblers all night long; at dawn
lay there, dumb
as the world's wood or winter,
no volcanic man.

Tears are an only poem.
I spread out
like a blind fakir, on the mat of the mind
sorry magic;
two scored stones for eyes,
broken sticks for limbs;
for man—
sans eyes, sans hands, a century's
empty locust shell.
For oracle, only
be content, be like.

THE DIVIDED MAN
CELEBRATES HIS BIRTHDAY

Come passionately into life,
inhabit the world
like a beloved body, intact, invaded.

Alas, no; man lives
neither caught up in Danae's cloud
nor taking joy of some fierce sacrifice;
but sodden, unlovely,
half murdered or born, dragged to his hour.

IN MEMORIAM (II)
(*G.M.*)

A young priest, dead suddenly
at forty years
taught a metaphysic of the world.
His mind was lucid, ingrained. He would say,
it is deductably verified
that God is immutable; and,
universal order converges on one being.

So be it. This priest, alas for poetry, love and priests
was neither great nor evil.
The truths he spoke
being inert, fired no mind to a flare;
a remote world order
of essence, cause, finality,
invited submission to his God.

He never conveyed a man, Christ, or himself—
His cleric's eye
forbade singulars, oddments, smells,
sickness, pushcarts, the poor.
He dwelt in the fierce Bronx, among a university's
stone faced acres
hemmed in by trucks and tumbrels. No avail.

Yet it could not be borne
by those who love him, that having passed
from unawareness to light
he should be denied
the suffering that marks man
like a circumcision, like unstanched tears; *saved.*

Heaven is everything earth has withheld.
I wish you, priest, for herald angel,
a phthisic old man

beating a tin can with a mutton bone—
behold he comes!

For savior,
unsavory men
a wino's dime
a Coxey's army, a Bowery 2 A.M.
For beatific vision
an end to books, book ends, unbending minds,
tasteless fodder, restrictive order.

For eternal joy
veins casting off, in a moment's
burning transfiguration
the waste and sludge of unrealized time.

Christ make most of you!
stitch you through
the needle's eye, the grudging gate.
Crawl through
that crotch of being;
new eyes, new heart, the runner's burning start.

ASTONISHMENT

Wonder
        why illness
an odious plague dispersed,
settles again after deep knives made
of the loved face a tragic mask.

Wonder
        why after one
tentative promise
raised like a green denial of death,
life resumes
its old mortician method after all.

Wonder
        why men break
in the kiln, on the wheel; men made of the sun,
men sprung from the world's cry; the only men,
literal bread and wine, the crucial ones
poured out, wasted among dogs. Wonder.

And the lees of men, the stale men, there
in the fair vessels, a mock feast;
take it or leave—nothing else in the house.

Wonder
        at omnipresence of grey minds,
the shade that made
O years ago, ash of the rowdy world.

Wonder
        at incapacity of love;
a stern pagan ethic, set against Christ at the door
(the discomfiting beggar, the undemanding poor).

Wonder
        woman and man, son and father
priest and sacrifice—to all right reason
one web of the world, one delicate
membrane of life. Ruptured.

Wonder.
Transcendent God does nothing.
The Child plays
among stocks and stones
A country almanac
records
moon phase, sun phase
hours and elements, grey dawn and red;
He sleeps and stands again,
moony, at loss, a beginner in the world.
History makes much of little; but He
of clay and Caesars, nothing.
There is no god in Him. Give us burly gods
to pummel the world and us, to shake its tree
quail and manna at morning!

Wonder, wonder,
                across his eyes
the cancerous pass unhealed, evil
takes heart monstrously. What use
the tarrying savior, the gentle breath of time
that in beggars is contentious and unruly,
that in dumb minds comes and chimes and goes
that in veins and caves of earth
sleeps like a tranced corpse, the abandoned body
of violated hope?

Wonder
given such God, how resolve the poem?

POPE PAUL GOES TO JERUSALEM;
THE MONA LISA AND THE PIETA
GO TO NEW YORK

If geography's the tip of someone's
scholastic needle, we'll ripen and rot there.
But life? Mona Lisa tries her luck
in treacherous waters. The innocuous stare

warms, her body cleaves the waters
like time's ripe swan. And Pieta, too long
in stale unanswering air; *whose sorrow
like mine?* Lady, we've not lived as long

in churches, but we die too, in droves.
In Queens meadow raise your eyes
from classic grief. The dead
bury the dead, and deep. Come walk our streets. Like Paul

the sun almost destroyed, that white moth.
He sweated under the cross, the raving
combustible crowd, a hanging or crowning mood.
In dreams, the living eat his flesh, his blood runs
nightlong, a staved cask in those alleys.

My dream beats on. I see the dead
in naked majesty, consumed with longing
for what we in the common street have by heart;
the leaf's errant fall, a child's cry. Delicate,
brutal, impure, pure—the world, the world
breaks them apart.

MAN IS AN ABYSS, AUGUSTINE CRIED

I saw wild hate and wilder love
murderous, uncontained,
race like a nightmare tumbrel by.

In that fury—
one man of compassion
tossed by chance or providence
among brute beasts;
I am here. What can do hurt
did all the world, at hell's nod, put on
black jaws, cleft hooves, a consonance of beasts?

Adam or Christ, or both;
one face redeems the world.
I saw each stand to the other—
man's folly, man transfigured—
a sinner's sweat
red on the holy face. Father Adam
exulting, topping the savior tree.

AND HE FED THEM ALL

That throng
Christ had worked wonders for—

the gentle blind
hearing like fauns
the fall of leaf, the hunters mindless will—

the halt
like marvelous broken statuary;

they come for eucharist, as though rumor ran
in grim autumnal streets
long cold, long unfed

of miraculous loaves and fishes among the dead.

TALISMAN

I wear
for sign of debt
a silver medal of Christ
sterile of flower or word,
itself time's flower
molten and hard; face incised
in the years' acid,
a savior's eye
sleepless, surviving man.

I wear it, a weakling
who kisses the knees of the strong man he fears
and in the dust, may yet
arise to love.

The face turns full profile away—
from time's stinking silver, Judas' kiss?

But a chain swings the rabbi full about.
The face is become
a savior's change of heart.
He turns to me.
I may yet
if silver outlast flesh

die unhanged in bed,
bought, sold for silver.

YOU TOO, BY THE SEA

Life; a vast knot of stinking
wet net, no nimble fingers to undo it,
no chanty to sing why, no fish
headlong, bullheaded to jump in and be

my congregation, my fish course—
No. But blue Monday by the sea.

The addled buoys dong bad luck by heart,
the sea stinks like a shored shark
malice in his man's jaw—*one more, only one more.*

Tired anger, bone weariness
colorless, graceless, dumb—

Nevertheless, the fisherman casts off

as if on sea
(or heart, or forehead)
an artery forked and ran—

a god's trident raking out
like sea lightning
some uncharted tragic way.

IF

If I am not built up
bone upon bone
of the long reach and stride of love—

if not of that
as stars are of their night;
as speech, of birth and death; thought
a subtle paternity, of mind's eye—

if not, nothing.
A ghost costs nothing.
Casts nothing, either; no net,
no fish or failure, no tears like bells

summoning across seas
the long reach and stride of love
dawning, drowning those black waters.

I ENCOUNTER MEN IN THE WORLD

   hopelessness stands in their eyes,
dry despair, hands broken upon stones,
eroded lives

I think then, of a young mother
her child in arms
a concentrated inwardness
as of a sea shell coiled, its music
self-composed, self-given.

I long at sight of illness to induce
—as a shell drawn from seas
generative, uncorrupted—
some birth their tears had not dared come upon.

YEAR OF OUR LORD
(*Algeria, 1961*)

Purest act fails. Imagination, trust,
spontaneity, heart's saving warmth, where?

I walk out, appalled
by day or night.
Somewhere a man dies in the camera's eye;
carrion dogs sniff, shy, prowl.
I long to stand in that picture, to kneel and drink
at a god's fountainhead.

World spins like a headless top,
butchers put up their shutters,
Caesar in dreams sucks red thumbs clean.

THE SISTINE CHAPEL

Illusory, a maelstrom of wrong purpose.
I would whitewash the whole.
Then, in favor of religion,
place there
for a poverello's sake
for his gospel eye, Cezanne's *Card Players*, say.

See, the painter cries, *God
is that meditative peasant
or the watcher brooding over; He is
like us, all said.*

Divine things
need only look human. The cards deal and fall
fair as leaves or creation; we are in good hands.

SORROW

I saw a mother
mourning her sick child
the hundredth time that day
or any day or night
equally wearying, equally hopeless.
She sees death stand at the end of days.

And saw a young husband;
his wife, suddenly dead, borne to the church door,
he, serving at Mass
impassive, cold at wrist and heart
to match her cold, one ice laid on one flesh.

The exemplary world moves us to tears
that in their falling, purify
eye's glance, impure world, both.

I know the world now, if world has face.
It beats steadily as a child's heart.
It is the moon's rhythm
that like a woman's long
unutterable glance of love
draws the bridegroom after.

SONG
(from Jacopone Da Todi)

In my morning prayer
I saw *love* written
upon every creature

men on their foreheads
trees on their leaves
houses on their walls.

Christ has flowered in man's flesh
let human nature rejoice!

PRAGUE: OLD WOMAN IN THE STREET

In the country saying, she was only
doing what must be done, as a stone falls
or a wheel turns; punished
by a man's labors, to man's shape.

Childbearing done, not for twilight peace
but for this; pulling a cart, sweeping cobbles
stolid in the killing cold. Suffering?
hands were made for it, blood warmed to it.

I tell you, I stood stupefied
as though a flare went up in the foul street,
some ikon Christ casting rags off for glory.

Woman I never knew, I kneel,
I am born of you. For you, my heart keeps
like an unhealed leper's, stint of hope—

Christ is not hard as stone, cold as my doubt.
You neared. Unbearably, the quick dead cried out.

FOR IVAN MESTROVIC

(his statuary; Jesus and the woman at the well)

Old epitaphs
chipped by ice and fever
falling to no use—

Nevertheless, rejoice to see
imagination
catch in vials
the last breath of the dead

to make of air an eye, of wind an ear,
of space, articulated arm and hand
to pluck the dead by the hair, to stand, to push them toward.

I saw in Notre Dame park the old man on his stick
pausing upon bronze Christ, thirsting upon His thirst.
No source could slake him; no, though the woman's vessel
were a human heart; its salt sweet,
its water wine, under that bridegroom's word.

MOMENT

Is the world then, more
than an animal haunch, cleft
under the butcher's ax,
a world hung raw, flayed on a hook?

Is the world more? is it
five or six deer together, standing in dusk
abstract, momentary; then startled, dissolved in
newer and newer rhythms, mauve hoofs, red nostrils
eyes unwary as first stars?

Are we, the watchers
bathed in that sight, a baptism?
The world
for all its stern exactions, loved us once:

homeward in dark, pondering *what is the world?*

A YOUNG BIRD FOUND DYING, BROUGHT INDOORS

                    The bird
never mastered air, and of earth
drew in no health, but a foul humor—
now lies blackening
and dead childish thing
untried by the world.

Earth mother—
tender, plangent, taking all to breast,
(children, great heroes, beauty, intellect)—

so slight a soul
lies light in a ghost's hand. Grant it
breath, passage to morning;
a furious phoenix brightening of hell.

HOW STRANGE THE WORLD

Richness, strangeness, depth; I see
autumnal birds in woodgrain;
the heart's skin, thin as sight
vatic as drumskin;
a drummer's ten fingers,
love, hate, brushfire, beaching of that scow
crammed like a pod with seed of
universal hope, animal and man—

the fingers; ten stars, conflagrations, seas—
I ride on them.

DACHAU IS NOW OPEN FOR VISITORS

The arabesque scrawled by the dead
in their laborious passage,
leaf and flower mould of their spent bodies,
faces frost touches
gently and coldly
to time's geometric—

a multitude of skeletal men
presses forward; such cries
the patient poor speak, whose despair
leaves no man's peace intact, no coin
for death's foreclosing fist.

IN THE CHILDREN'S WARD

I was pondering no mystery
and far in mind from mystery's
Necromancer who, time gone,
made five flowers grow
in consecrated ground,
lit five candles in a ghost's hands and feet.

Merciful men and women stood appalled
when the Lord sank and died; a crowned head
must, if it rise intact
make a fiery circle around; all
stand without.

I thought as I bent
to innocent blind faces
how inmost sight refused my face; linen
ripped like graverot; eyes
no tears burned black, met mine.
And pity died—the feeble child
my childish nightmare made
of rickety bed and doll.

All, all wrong.
Sight was blind. But the children
moved dexterous as fireflies, in a blind
garden of broken hands and dull minds.

I FEAR MOST, I THINK

    if nightmare is oracle—
not madman death
not quartan fevers
nor the long litany hell composes
of unstrung jaws, their fiery diatribe

but dreaming or waking—
that child
pale as mushroom, blind as night fog

no grace, no stance, no name—
shuddering, lame, befouling the world.

HOLY COMMUNION
(*for Michael*)

The lidless spider at ceiling
gathered no moss, alert in gloom—
hunger, cold, the ugly staved room.

O if the threads broke, the spider
leapt like a hunchback cretin free
and the net swam down murderous—
would the cup then
make miracles for Christ's crew

that is childish in the world, that escapes
day upon day, hell's ambush by a hair?

I stand there steady,
broken bread in hands.
Was it spider thread
or light, light, on dead eyes
crossed my eyes? Lazarus
a moment, did not know, and knew.

THE POEM

When I see flowers borne into a city room
I am urged inward—
the gross slag, filth and mire
to the heart of life.

Amplitude, warmth, saving compassionate grace—
the flowers beat and beat on. The divine ship;
silken and tough in the wind, it
beats and beats on. The poem
is the journey toward.

LAST DAY

When He came, all the
folderol in the books burned like faces
for shame. *Imagine the world*
not catching fire, that no other
reason or being, preachers cried like frogs.

Not a sleeper's hair turned, not one.
Where the living dwelt, He took breath; where the dead
lay cold as stones, or stood, long stones on end,
He troubled none alive. They were safe from Him.

It was more like the sun's fiery mind
or a woman's hands, compassion. Not one
dull standing autumn weed denied

its windless hour, warmth and seed. He was not named
   storm.

LINES

Excellence, holiness,
radiant style of life, all
liable to process
of inert minds; trial by epithet,
execution by irony, burial by despisal;
overmastering fear of action, time
gutted of substance and surprise;
protest and anger
dead in the human furrow

and love, great love, who is the heart's
daystar and oracle,
whose teasing marvel is
touch me and be,
who walks the bestiary mind
lion and lamb, man and woman, one—

great love forbidden utterance and act.

> This tears me, as wild horses
> in a mad dream ran wrecking.
> Or worse—in a dream of waking, stood
> horrible, at large, real in the world.

Paris Suite

1. A BEGGAR, FIRST

Sometimes, misery has beauty to commend it.
I saw a poor man bedding down
in the midnight street, coolly. He might have been
gorgeous Louis preparing levee.

Weather stood austere,
late goers homeward, pinched, intent.
The beggar made his bed as best
rags, leaves, torn paper might. De Gaulle's

disgruntled snowman face
crumpled under head, made a pillow
like ambergris
floating the brain gently nightlong

in a grand savory sauce
of power and rhetoric. Human life
flickers inextinguishably in the jungle street.
The beggar, annealed in dignity

settles back
in rags his dignity weaves new.
He takes up in cold hands
tattered Molière: Those cunning civilized hands

that lifted, veil on veil
the quintessential ironies of mind,
that fleeced the rich to very clout, that hailed
great Jove in rags—

    crown him at midnight.

2. OUR LADY OF PARIS

Mother of exodus, her cold hands take
of this world no comfort

Tonight, stinking Seine
leaps the quay stones, takes living flesh
in morsels. A gypsy
mother and child might dream
four walls and fire; and Mary
white faced at door for shelter.
Always, the poor—

Dives screams in his stews,
his tripod of burning bones.

3. CONCESSIONS

You are not the golden Greek sea, no
Shakespeare never slept here—
granted, the nightingale is heard
only in Versailles tapestry;

starting with stern exclusions
I end as always
helpless in praise;
marvelous architect of man; mind's life that
transubstantiates to poetry.

Cast words away. The city, the
egg of Venus, halves into all things.

4. SAINT SULPICE

In the botched barracks, coming on
a marvelous suave Christ; thigh to wrist, one line
of contending death and life, the wood
golden as time's honeycomb—
                              stuck out of sight for
being guilty of beauty
                        as though in some
grimy back yard, a scarecrow stood
and withstood, and in spring arose
caparisoned as Spring Christ with trumpet vine.

5. UNFINISHED LINES

A bronze head of Mallarmé by Picasso—
the true burden of falling leaves.
Does man live only in thought? Where are his hands?

Why ask? Great lines crown the brow
that crowns its quiet grove.

But how clasp hands with the dismembered dead?

No one's familiar. Listen and look long.

6. PARIS, YOU COULD PRESS WINE FROM THISTLES

make easter eggs of gutter stones.
Your metaphysical butchers chop and chop,
time's neat headsmen. Irony and grace
hold like a lifted shrug, all life in fee.

What unlikely thing is not your poem?
one leaf in Luxembourg gardens
trodden, dried, a simian brown.
But hold it up; a fan, a lover's lattice
to say through to the world
if you stand there in brown twilight, I love you.

7. A VIEW FROM A SIDE STREET

The streets
        shouldering awkwardly along
like flower carts
all sight and bestowal—

windows like blank eyes
starved
for one burning realizing blue—

Walk out
some night
        that sacks your sight,
a condemned man's,
           in suffocating black.

Be lucky,
      a star falls,
           cry out *I see.*

8. A THRUSH IN THE CITY

Supple as a fish
or a violinist's hands
the thrush
fans out, ascends,
paying to gravity
the tribute of grace

not as a parasite
I drink of you earth mother
but standing at height
to pour from a gold mask
poetry on your wounds

9. THE CITY UNDERTAKES A RESTORATION OF PUBLIC MONUMENTS

To admit death and beginning

taking that blow like any woman
her brow wet
with birth or death sweat, she scarce
knows. *How much life?* she mocks death.

I would in the wandering city
make in my mind that phrase
new, anew; despite
time's cruelties, that belabor

innocent men, clear expectancies.
How much life? I seek.
Algerian workmen
with steam hoses, burnish new
the scarred animate bones of Paris.

10. THE NEWSSTAND

In cold November
the old man stood
all day
in a flimsy canvas box,
struts, patches;
       a lung, a world
billowing with big portentous names.
The stone man stood;
       drumming like a god
wars, death,
       time's bloodletting and getting.

At sundown
       the world came apart,
a shack of cloth and board
          roped, hefted.
Last, rolled up his pages;
       the leonine faces
snuffed without cry,
       dead as all day.

11. IMMANENCE

I see You in the world—
venturesome children, their cries and gestures,
the sharp sad whistle at six, the emptying park,
flybitten leaves, embers of the magnificent
weathered candelabra, the poplar lanes.

Yet faith asks, like a shaky woman, some epiphany—
a renaissance cock calling Peter's sin
from the Pantheon roof, shocking the crowd's ease,
sinking the children's fleet

that now make alas, as life does, a silly wayward wake
or none at all; and no one walks waters.

12. AIR MAIL LETTER

That mysterious lord
ikons and saints speak of
seldom if ever deigns
miracles, interventions.

I saw once, a procession
of halt, blind nuns;
on Corpus Christi day
they wove of flowers and leaves
their *tao*, their adoration

Dark fell; the nuns'
bodies swung like vanes.
Their eyes
triumphant, ravaged, held
life's acid ironies.

I carried the Host that day.
They in the doorway singing
floated midstream;
a foil of swanlike forms

Then
(no warning)
steeled upright, turned
intent, unappeased, to me.
Come cried the virgins *despise*
vain emulation, the childish
time-ridden heart. Bring to birth
in one flush of being
intelligence and love.

The moment passed. Twelve
defeated women, singing
Pange Lingua. Slowly
entered again the dark
portal of horn or ivory.

These occurred to me—
gentle adherence, love,
hope beyond reason of hope.

THIS BOOK

As I walk patiently through life
poems follow close—
blind, dumb, agile, my own shadow,
the mind's dark overflow, the run of vein
we thought red once, but know now, no.

Poem called death
is unwritten yet. Some day will show
the last line first
the shadow rise,
a bird of omen

snatch me for its ghost

and a hand somewhere,
                          purposeful as God's
close like two eyes, this book.

V

FALSE GODS, REAL MEN

FALSE GODS, REAL MEN

1.

Our family moved in 25 years from Acceptable Ethnic
through Ideal American
    (4 sons at war   Africa   Italy   the Bulge   Germany)
and Ideal Catholic
    (2 sons priests   uncle priest   aunt nun   cousins
                           great-uncle   etc.   etc.)
But now; 2 priests in and out of jail, spasms, evictions,
                                confrontations

    We haven't made a nickel on the newest war
    probably never again
                   will think, proper
    with pride; a soldier! a priest! we've made it now!

What it all means is—what remains.
    My brother and I stand like the fences
        of abandoned farms, changed times
        too loosely webbed against
                deicide   homicide
    A really powerful blow, a cataclysm
        would bring us down like scarecrows.
    Nature, knowing this, finding us mildly useful
        indulging also
        her backhanded love of freakishness
            allows us to stand.

    The implication
        both serious and comic;
            wit, courage
        a cry in the general loveless waste

something
        than miracle
                both more and less

. . . did conspire to enter, disrupt, destroy
draft files of the American Government, on
the 17 day of May . . .
                                —Indictment

2.

Among the flag poles
wrapped like Jansenist
conventicles
with rags
at half mast
(alas for sexual
mortmain) the wooden poles
on high but
dry

3.

We did yes we did your Honor
impenitent—
while legitimate cits
newts   bats   foxes
made congress
in formerly
parks and green swards
rutting   earnestly drilling
tooth and claw
galling   inserting
industrious   inventive
nitroglycerin, nuclear
instrumentalities

4.

We fools and felons
went on a picnic
apples   quince   wines   hams   swimsuits
loaves   fishes   noonday relics and traces
badminton   watery footsoles   infants all
thereafter impounded!

> An FBI agent estimated at least 600 indi-
> vidual files were in the two huge wire bas-
> kets carried from Local Board No. 33 and
> set fire in the parking lot.
>
> —AP dispatch

5.

Then foul macadam
blossomed like rosemary
in the old tapestry
where unicorns deigned
to weave a fantasy
truer I swear than

6.

Judge Mace his black
shroud   his skeletal
body & soul
whose veins decant
vapors to turn the
innocent eye
dry as the dead.

7.

Indicted
charged with creating
children   confusion
legerdemain   flowers
felonious picnics.
Jews in Babylon
we sit and mourn
somewhere in Mace's
mad eyes' space

8.

TO PHILIP

Compassionate, casual as a good face
(a good heart goes without saying)
someone seen in the street; or
infinitely rare, once, twice in a lifetime

that conjunction we call brother or friend.
Biology, mythology cast up clues.
We grew together, stars made men
by cold design; instructed

sternly (no variance, not by a hair's
breadth) in course and recourse. In the heavens
in our mother's body, by moon and month
were whole men made.
We obeyed then, and were born.

OBIT

We die

showing like frayed pockets, space within
without, for loss.
                         Pain in eyes, a ragged
animal before the gun;
                       muzzily—
can death do any harm
life hasn't done? maybe
                      (dreamily) *death*
turns old dogs
into fish hillsides butterflies
              teaches a new
trick or two

THIS CRUCIFIX

Where great love is
are miracles, the saints say
who are held
in principle, to no proof.

No
its man
clings there, life's last straw
death's
crude analogate.

Cold man
we push the gospel
at a dead heart.

No proof. Day after day I turn
to cry the healer for some hint.
From dying eyes
there flies
a sliver cock
to taste the bitter air

foul   foul.
and someday—*fair?*

*The following twelve poems were written on
the spot, in the course of a trip to Hanoi,
January 31–February 18, 1968.*

*References to actual persons, living or dead,
are purely intentional—indeed willful.*

WAITING: VIENTIANE

The birds of dawn are crying, drawing
                    the great sun into conflict
            a contested light

the bloody challenge taken, the spurred leap, roof after roof.

            Visualize such a bird
        as you imagine the sun
                        a black carapace
                        a fruit bitter as limes
                            a bull studded with flags
        a guerrilla striking while the iron is hot.

            SUN
                who alone cocks eye (eyeing that cock)
                            and not
                    burns his socket blind; from that
        intolerable equinox, seeing in the sea
                    himself rampant, eye to eye
            lives in that cry

                    nor turns to stone
                            nor no, shall die

PRAYER

I left Cornell
with half a wit; six mismated socks
ski underwear, a toothbrush,
passport, one hundred good
green dollars, their faces
virtuous as ancestors,
the chamois sack
Karl Meyer gave me years ago, handmade
by dispossessed Georgia Negroes.

Later, dismay; no Testament.
I must construct, out of oddments, abrasions,
vapor trails, dust, pedicabs
three crosshatch continents, Brooks Brothers embassies
their male models dressed to kill—

all He meant and means. I touch
shrapnel and flesh, and risk my reason
for the truth's sake, an ignorant hung head.

Man of one book, stand me in stead.

NIGHT FLIGHT TO HANOI

In a bar in Vientiane
they said to us
like Job's mockers;
thanks to your own ever loving bombers
you may never see
the northern lights, Hanoi.

Then, by bat radar
we crawled that corridor
blind as bats,
a wing and a prayer.

Came in!
the big glare of a klieg eye
held us, hooked, death's open season.
We held breath, fish
baited, not landed.

Ended; the pale faces of flowers
said suddenly, out of season
something than death other, unuttered.

Exiles we went in
safe kept, cherished by strangers.

ALERT

The sirens are loosed on Hanoi
a Stalingrad
ringed round, rained upon, fired—

the air force calls
like a whistle of game cocks at dawn
like a song of songs
like the embassy eagle
on whom the sun never sets
the celibate, the almost
      (for self will
       for lack of an equal
       killer or climber)

extinct of its kind.

BOMBARDMENT

Like those who go aground
willfully, knowing that man's
absurd estate can but be bettered
in the battering hands of the gods—

yet mourning traitorously the sun and moon
and one other face, and heat of hearth—

went under
like a blown match. The gases flare on the world's combustible
flesh.

CHILDREN IN THE SHELTER

Imagine; three of them.

As though survival
were a rat's word,
and a rat's death
waited there at the end

and I must have
in the century's boneyard
heft of flesh and bone in my arms

I picked up the littlest
a boy, his face
breaded with rice (his sister calmly feeding him
as we climbed down)

In my arms fathered
in a moment's grace, the messiah
of all my tears. I bore, reborn

a Hiroshima child from hell.

FLOWERS

A flower is single jeopardy—
only one death; matrons' scissors, dogs,
natural deflowering; choose! Meantime
dare time and wind and war. Be

no one's metronome, discount
in a lover's hand, the ways
we die—routine, wrong analogy.

I start these words because
a girl on a bicycle
swaying

bears a few flowers
homeward through war, a double jeopardy.
I held
breath for her, her flowers, on the wheel of fire,
the world, no other.

Sentries, we passed, no countersign

except *good-bye*
forced   first   last word of all.

SONG

The maids sing at their scrubbing
the cooks at the stove—

shame, women; such lightness of mind
ill becomes; think rather on
Death   Judgment   Heaven   Hell

the names of the bombers
that bear in their skull
your names, memorized in fire.

PROGRESS IN RURAL DEVELOPMENT:
A LECTURE ON PRIVIES,
AND A GIFT TO OUR COUNTRYMEN

In the municipal hospital, in the bone-chilling cold
the dispassionate voices, Viet and English, unfolded
an invincible case for improvement of village privies.

Doubters, we sniffed with our senses the odorless faeces
achieved by new methods of drying. We stood.
The photographer readied. Passed to the doctor's hands

and to ours, and on through ten thousand miles
into marveling America (and carefully constructed
as a boat in a bottle, as a model of Model T)
       that gift, that two-seated wonder.

MY NAME

If I were Pablo Neruda
or William Blake
I could bear, and be eloquent

an American name in the world
where men perish
in our two murderous hands

Alas Berrigan
you must open those hands
and see, stigmatized in their palms
the broken faces
you yearn toward

you cannot offer
being powerless as a woman
under the rain of fire—
life, the cover of your body.

Only the innocent die.
Take up, take up
the bloody map of the century.
The long trek homeward begins
into the land of unknowing.

THE PILOTS, RELEASED

1.

When I think of you it is always (forgive me)
of disposable art; 50 designs, the damp woodcut
of 50 States, the physiognomy of camp—

Innocence (mom), *pietas* (pop), the household gods
guarding the gates guarded by you, O proxies
for all providence   Saigon to

Rio to Congo   your chilling logic
draws blood   a blood bank   a blank bloody
check drawn on the living
                              who thereupon
      here   there   and tomorrow by all accounts
                are dead

2.

The trouble with innocence
is itself, itself in the world—
the GI who had a wife
but never imagined one
had children true to form
whose lives described
like dance or geometry
the outer edge, drawn there
in diametric blood—
thus far love, and no further.

THERE MUST BE A GOD

I thought I heard
my own life say it
and the crumbling streets
and alkys mumbling, and the shot landscape
of my youth; *gone—*
trees, sweetness, euphoria

Yet in hair or hand
a rose, blown, ragged,
a victory somewhere
like a torch in the hands of a runner
beat, dying, but on his feet.

Let there be a God!
is man's big news;
let Him show as much heart
as a good man musters;
leave us alone
to make do, fumble about, fret through;
He must leave us our sins
to learn and ravel;
sweat, start false, feint, dissimulate.

Let Him be a dying vine, a back door
marked "colored only"
day old bread, wino's wine.
Let Him "stand with the fate
of the majority of men."
A shepherd, if he likes folklore,
like the Roman gypsies
at Christmas time
blowing their big sheep bladders
like an ass's brag
crying, not Christmas
but their own sores and rags.

O incarnation is a hard word.
There is some flesh I could not take.
On my way to a Bowery wedding
the Bowery sty;
in a Bellevue ward
sour lees, sour wine;
uptown east, spiffy aseptic dogs
parading cloud nine;
the doormen's preternatural fishy stare—

ah wilderness! He marvels
I am more astonished
with what I find here
than with what I bring!

THE CLOCK IN THE SQUARE
REMINDS ME OF CERTAIN LIVES

Ineffectuals
chained, reined to time's beaten track—
simulacra all, strangers to action, passion

strike the hour, lurch away
pale as linen
the pharaohs of long refusal.

SOME SORT OF EXPLANATION,
BETTER THAN NONE

I cultivate a grin
that takes into account
a rear end
bruised
by an ass's iron shoe

Meantime
that knock you hear
is death's drumstick
tapping his forehead 3 times
with the knowing look
of woody woodpecker;

for this, and other
prudential courtesies
    of wind & weather
    of lack and luck
    of the fair fall
    of bones them bones—

love life!

SOMEHOW

I kiss a book sometimes
like a bride or the gospel
or land, after wild seas
grant me a man again.

The things we love!
women, the truth, planets—

like flowers through ruins
like brides through deserts
like shore through murderous mist—

out of wreckage and rancor. Somehow!

COME ALIVE (on the Long Island Railroad)

I had lost everything for a year
a stick in a blind hand—
conundrums, fantasy

the blind hand struck, the stick
stuck rotting in rich ground.
Four seasons come and gone.

Imagine a face? summon
sustenance, vision, up from that ground?

My mind took no fire
from fiery truth; my hands hung
like hanged necks, dead, dead as a show.

But the children of Birmingham
clairvoyant, compassionate among the dead—

I see you all night long.
Dawn winds freshen. The cock
makes children by the clock.
The trees lift up their dawn.

SOMEWHERE THE EQUATION
BREAKS DOWN

between the perfect
                              (invisible, Plato said)
and the imperfect
                      that comes at you on the street,
                      stench and cloth and fried eyes;
between the wired bones of the dead
                                      stuttering, shamed
and the marvelous lucid spirit
                          that moves in the body's spaces
                          a rainbow fish behind glass—
      decide. O coincide!

NOVEMBER 20, 1965

Subway faces beheaded
in the blade of your eyes.
Life? step in, be
lost.
All heaven's bells
nod in accord
like Botticelli curls;
yes O yes

I think of my father and mother;
their dignity measures
the horror—
that leap
marked like a third rail's
mortal sputter;
danger!

They leapt, and live;
the stranger's wounds succored
the lost child safe in arms.

I WONDER, DO YOU

    know
the things you make seem
    possible?
  My flesh ends; be-
  neath, a toehold on hell;
ahead, a divining rod; above
    a hairy
  pumpkin with a grin
    knifed in.
  Life; my cry, your gift
      —else
   head to feet, I
rot like fish in voracious air;
    the rod that greened and perked
 on rumor of fresh springs
     die
  like an issueless king's
   dry stick, wet dream

PEACEMAKING IS HARD

(Jim and Sally)

   hard almost as war.
The difference being one
we can stake life upon
and limb and thought and love.

I stake this poem out
dead man to a dead stick
to tempt an Easter chance—
if faith may be
truth, our evil chance
penultimate at last

not last. We are not lost.

When these lines gathered
of no resource at all
serenity and strength,
it dawned on me—

a man stood on his nails

as ash like dew, a sweat
smelling of death and life.
Our evil Friday fled,
the blind face gently turned
another way, toward life

a man walks in his shroud

THE TRIP

It was a foolish ricochet
of ignorance off good intention.
I came on the New Haven railroad
to visit a friend in Darien Hospital.
The New Haven
is like the emergency room
of a public hospital, the close
of a catastrophic day.

So it seemed that day.
Innocent, feckless, men
hawked their wares
with overkill drunken skill;
all, all aboard; no haven.

The New Haven; four sailors
(I am accident prone)
staked their claim near me.
One of them strummed a guitar,
a passable voice.
They worked through ten or twelve
gentle songs.
Then things turned around, turned ugly;
the songs, the air
sour as a drunk's distemper.

I hope
I am not grown hopeless
seeing things often go
from ripe to rot.
That ripeness they say is all—
how rare!

sometimes, toward dawn, it comes—
a hand like my father's hand
brown, veinous, streaked
pops
the first prize Farmer's Pride
into my mouth.
I eat
as much as a man eats
whose life, a free load,
bodes ill, brings in
no harvest cash.

SEMINAR

One speaker
an impeccable
Californian
impelled to explain

The Chinese Belong In China
The Russians In Russia.
we however—
messiah, oversoul
a pink   muscled   clear-eyed
Texan dream
fumigating
Hanoi privies
from above—
napalm   jigger bombs   gas
God's saniflush, in sum—

The gentleman was
four square as State
or the pentateuch;
sans beard, rope sandals, foul talk, pot—
a fire extinguisher
on Pentecost day;
exuding good will
like a mortician's convention
in a plague year.

Indeed yes.
There is nothing sick
(the corpse said)
about death.
Come in.

WALLS

The wall
stood like an old sarge
flat-footed   blank faced   clipped

bellowing orders—
Privies to clean!
Murders for sale!
(somebody's taxes paid for somebody's fevers)

thus
behind every window a candle
behind every soldier a mother
knitting

death heads into shawls
behind every wall
surprise!   another wall

except when you   Corita
create a smile
where no face was   and
ready!   aim!
barks from the mastiff mouth

The wall
turns to water
runs   runs like a miler
                    to hell out of here and man

A HARD DAY IN THE CITY,
FOLLOWED BY FUN AND GAMES
(*for S.S.*)

One would have thought
breeding, money, a swimming pool out back
and running free, 5 beautiful children

would compensate—but what?

the price our lives
like it or not, exact; other forms and smells

cast in the face, than roses.

O nights ago
when lightning broke
we ran like demons
300 yards to the columned shelter
the big house furred, lit like a st. bernard's eyes

across the sweet grass, ran
from sight, from sightlessness
          our desperate hearts' last dash

AN OLD WIFE REMEMBERS

We started in a clapboard house that year
on a turnpike next to a Cutty Sark sign.
The bottle stood up, big as a bum's dream.

He'd say; just wait, tonight after ten you'll see.

Well yes. The bottle lit up, started,
tipped, poured light like a firebrand
I thought, the Empire State Building
tumbling on you, millions of goodies,
the water coolers, the heating plant, look out!

O the visual aids we had that year!

The light crossed his brows
red then green, a go ahead. We went under, gently, fiery.

There was a story somewhere—
trolls lived under a waterfall, boys trod a furnace. You
O you were mine.

1967—VIETNAM

Two hands (fixation, horror)
raised in the stone doorway
falter, let drop
wine and fire from the empty cup.

You avail—nothing.

Something? tell
the bread that failed, the circuses that fell.

TRIP THROUGH MICHIGAN

The poem started,
Pure in a time of toads,
a jewel in a pismire—

No. I mean to come
if time is merciful, to a simpler word

You; a vegetarian; *since I work among the poor*
and most men never taste meat!
Sleeping on the floor, glorying, brimming
like a Hebrew hero, a full vessel.
I thought of Blake's god,
touching the universe at all points,
a child within a hoop, light and exaltation;
a vine, groaning with life, a eucharist tree—
not a sour drop, nor sour ground
underfoot.

We drove the Michigan roads
like Jonahs in God's belly.
The moon came on like a prophet's lamp.
Behind, the neanderthals, their posters
"Judas" in red, three goons bearing a cross,
our meeting broken up like a puppet nightmare;
back to Wayne
marveling, bewildered, beat.

Life in the whale
big as an island cavel
We
pumping him on like a heart
pushing his lungs like a bellows

bound for a port
sealed like ambergris in some secret brain.

TURNING THE PICTURE BOOK
(a Eucharistic procession)

Your unreal presence in a photo, passed
down a Spanish street;
a long line of surpliced priests
receding.
One half the page was this;
an honor guard
bayonets massed, a street barricade.

Believe me, gorgeous bird
we were not hungry for your heart.
There you went
a millionaire's heir,
Prague's golden boy,
the Czar's easter egg,
a baby resembling bread.
And hell's angels,
your blank-eyed muscle men
keeping you safe
from a kidnapping.

O if I were you
I would strike them down
like Pilate's bullies
stand and break
myself in two
like Samson's heart
in his own hands. Myself,
like bread
like a hero's heart.

A CIVIL RIGHTS DEMONSTRATION

That morning I weighed
like a Dickens brat
no expectations. Would I march
capped in bells like Christ's fool, or Christ?

who walked with us
borne on what wind?
driven Jews, sere in vein and eye?
Sharpeville's seventy, brave in red ribbons?

O who will turn
dust to a man on march? I taste in mouth
the dust of Jews, the *durst not kill* of prophets
a taste that kills.

Bread loaf king
shelved, mouldering; a churchmice clergy start

cut, flee for cover. See how they run
like field mice under the teeth or scythe. Like men.

ON THE TURNPIKE

Who loaded history's pig iron
pack, bade a man shoulder it
and die of it and
                    if he could
rise in the shoddy world?

Thus; a monger man, his sack
big as shroud or sail, trailing
the stinking phosphorous waste.

I saw or half saw from the sky way stream
Dachau and Easter garden, a rag man
poking the filth for bread
                           heard
one lost word on that witch's wind
riding the vacuum, its own

good news or foul, who knows, a rose?

BERGAMO: Instructions for Going Forth

(News item:
*In a fresh dug crypt
under the new seminary,
they are constructing
a 2,000 seat church
against the day
when John XXIII of Bergamo
is declared saint.*)

1.

Alas if a man's death
toss his bones
like unlucky dice
among medicine men
hawkers spivs

might he not
cast a more thoughtful eye
on other
exits, intercessions?

Birds of paradise
long distance runners
acrobats   wandering clerks

invitations   dawns
catherine wheels
love poetry   death by fire

sandal wood pyres   ashes
borne upon streams
from the heartland
a land (at last) of no
morticians

GUESS WHAT I ALMOST LOST TODAY

A sidelong hairy look
a mouth like a silk purse—

he held it tight
in six-fingered hands

weighing the king's eyeballs,
honest though God be thief.

I got it back and breathed it in
safe and scarce.

It screwed its face to a fist
like a babe at the nipple

what did I mean in hell or heaven
bartering the unborn away

that way   without a vote?

THE WEDDING

(*for David and Catherine Miller*)

Make way, make way! the poor
sit for the wedding feast; syrup onions beans
a chunk of bread.
                          Guitars
strum it like throats; come to the marriage day!

And I thought; you must take it whole,
you must swallow it, acrid, disastrous,
the sour air, the clangor, the revolting
loveless, heartless, unjust mass,
weights pressing the heart into weird misshape,
the imponderable brutal load that makes
brutes of us all; neutral minds,
stocks and stones; rapacious ominous law
nine points of dispossession, faces
beaten under night sticks;
                          the churches
gripping like locust shells the tegument of life—

Don't speak of love until everything is
lost; antagonism, agony!
no vow, no faith, the wedding bread
spoiled, scattered like chaff; the bride
a whoring recusant.
                          O who will make
amends, my love?
                          I climbed up
step after iron step, inferno
into your eyes. I have married
sight of your face, that took
all this and me beside
                          for groom, for the bride's
evil and good, sickness and hope and health.

Yes.
    I have learned from you
                YES
                    when
                      no
unmans me like a knife, turns
like an evil lock, the incarnate bridal door.

DIARY (Easter, 1966)

I hadn't walked the tow path in Central Park
for six months, having flapped southward
like a lame duck, under circumstances
that yield here to self-censoring.

I left; the Park gave scarcely a shrug,
the big body
autumnal, luxuriant,
a vague disinterest in eye
a hung up blear of smog
a rare fitful candor, a dog's
intelligence, an old horse's look. O sun!

Absent, the Park was in my heart
not noble, remorseful, remembering;
a wink, a New York shrug.
Nevertheless, went with me
an animal shadow, all its animals—
seals, weeping
the absurdest tears of all creation—

I called good night
that last time, November 20. The sea lion
a shmoo's dream of beatitude, a feast afloat
turned on me
his rheumy uncle's eye;
time for all that
time to envy eagles, clouds like slow birds,
gulls slow as paper from the huffing stacks
time for return. He'd see me.

Southward, I thought of paeons to the Park.
Rio children had a park in mind
mud pies, dust cake, the hominoids like children.
Alas, their bones scrawled in the dust
alas, and the winds took the word away, as years
our bones

Home again, I visit the seal;
his majesty, cold in his ingrown mask
tight in his poorhouse trousers,
promulgates
the good life, laissez-faire,
49 brands of fish.

Ponderous
half in, half out of the water
his leather flipper
tapping the sea wall like God the Father
or Teddy Roosevelt
WELCOMES ME, NAME OF ALL!

O the Park descends on the city
like a celestial napkin, as if heaven
were all of earth, the fusty smell
of animals in arks, of cornered lives and deaths.
What is our freedom, Peter?
Obedience.
You have answered well;

I give you—exodus.
Wandering Jew
you have a Jew for God.
The Park
unreal as real estate
under the flood
bears you away, ashore:
The city!

JOHN ANDERSON MY JO JOHN

Men cannot pluck or wear
the mystery that bears no flower here;
or does, but we
no flowering eyes to see.

Yet take my flesh's word—
it roots in me, draws blood;
some death
or birth perhaps. I have no word.

A SAINT ON THE DASHBOARD:

    to hear. But not too near.
I had a friend once, failed
for dogged solicitude,
playing shadow, crawling in my skin.

Leave kids their sins.
Let them cut their sails
badly, toward shoals.
Better wrong
than tolled, right and left.
The saint
toils on as he toiled
the chancy road where he
like we, find or not
the white pebble under a toad's rot.

Life is the very devil.
Who needs a plastic conning smile
to say so or no?

A SEVERE CRITIC, A KIND OF ANSWER

Of course, violence!
the rose torn from its bush

color, form, defenselessness, all invite
    violation, celebration,
death, apotheosis, the breast of the beloved.

But it is one thing, you agree
    to pluck a flower
        as a large gracious way
    beyond, not tantamount to
words   words   words

And another;
    the iron mercenary stance
        of Bully Boy
    his mount
        letting go like Pantagruel

    a defoliant hissing
        over the rose beds

while with steely savior's eye
    astride the brutal shoulders
        our boy
scans the horizon for a bigger game.

SALVATION HISTORY

I had a nightmare—
the rickety shack brought down
I was sheltering in;
from sleep to death
gone, all coped in dream

What then? I had never lived?
it well might be.
Without friends, what is a man?
their noon and moon, my own

Without friends—what?
dead, unborn, my light
quenched, never struck.

The piteous alternatives
life simulates!
streets haunt, faces hang

but I mark
like an unquenched man
merciful interventions

a clean end or beginning
someone to die for   some love to sing

WEST SIDE STORY

A Broadway hash joint, a Puerto Rican
short orders *2 burgers with cheese,*
2 without; onions, ketchup

in 4 minutes flat, with style, verve, and
a rare smile in a sour borough.

Far from Gracie Mansion and the gentle Sheep
Meadow. He hasn't smelled roses in years

but he wears them. While
nightmares hustle like rats
a night's undoing
              he feeds modestly
(a few inferior loaves, a few
greasy fish) the city poor.

Winner? we have no other.
In a bad time, blessed
are you, for blessing me.

AND WHAT IS MAN

Not like the rich
a fist of worms for a heart;
nor like the poor
consumed with making do,
rancor at dawn, futility at dusk

say; like a slum child
in a filthy yard—
a spool, a few crossed sticks

something different from himself—
the doll wound on a bobbin
almost talks back,
almost stalks away.

Was this the way He meant us?
meddlesome
proud, not docile

to stand to Him, thwart, amaze Him still!

I AM NEVER COMPLETE

(*for Al and Barbara Uhrie*)

A man, a woman, their love
in the lower East Side
like Shakespeare added to
a sentient row of minds.
Make room, the books whisper.
The majestic mind, as they move
makes room for its counterparts.
I am never complete, history
awaiting its further emblem.
Among children, junkies, pushcarts
a lover's heart searches out my heart.

FACING IT

Who could declare your death,
obedient as Stylites, empty as death's head
majestic as the world's sun   moving
into night?

It was a hollow death; men
dread it like a plague. Thieves die this way,
charlatans, rejects. A good man's thought recoils;

to grow old yes,
home and faces
drifting out of mind. Abrupt violence yes
a quick mercy on disease

but not, not this; the mother's face
knotted, mottled with horror,

time's cruel harrowing
furies at the reins of fortune
wild horses dragging
the heroic dishonored body on time's ground.

O for an act of God! we cry, before death utterly
reduce to dust
          that countenance, that grace and beauty.

But
come wild hope, to dead end. War, murder,
anguish, fratricide.

No recourse. The case of Jesus Christ
is closed. Make what you will

desire, regret, he lies
stigmatized, a broken God
the world had sport of.

Risen? we have not turned that page.

TO THE PRISONERS

(*Mexico City*)

I saw the iron rings about the necks
of tortured prisoners
in frescoes by Rivera, in the National Palace.
Above, monkey-faced monks
held to the dying, the lying crucifix.

Behold, the iron on other necks now!
the cleric's collar, like a spiked mastiff
warns; *keep off*
color, music, sexual sweetness, spontaneity
passionate use of the world!
a black coverall
begins at wrists and ankles
like sacking on the dolls
that in my childhood, began to be true
at neck, hands and feet; all between
homunculus of straw, alas!

When they had locked the prisoners' irons
(the guide book says)
the executioners came forward
a line of purposeful apes
Platonic, implacable . . .

it is our history. In the mercado
you choose from a basket;
dolls' head, hands, feet
and in another booth
sacking and shredded straw
to fashion
a five-pointed rustling star
sew it to limbs
that walk, gesticulate—
a blank-eyed verisimilitude,
Tissot's still born first born.

Madame's son?
we will never know; the crotch
is decently stitched
sterile as an armpit.

Our testament forbids
(despite the murderous hands
that stain the text)
torture, murder, the bloody curriculum
taken like rare meat.
I stand apart from the fresco,
at the same time
I lie within it!
A friend, a psychologist
half serious, called me
his "troubled adolescent."
He found me
lightheaded in Mexican air
weeping
for organized madness
a half starved dog
guarding the dead flesh of my brother.
Better, I thought, among men, a dog
than among dogs, a killer.

Every day, every day, five years,
efficient as a madman's
five year plan
for renewal of the earth
the bombers go out
renewing the earth

And men adduce;
the onslaught of the beast
clairvoyance, civilized,
violent only under duress
"all recourse failing"—
he lights the way
with his dragon's breath.

Let all bow down   worship   follow,
it is meet and just.

Indeed, it is the genius
of the king of the beasts
to weave analogies
from superhuman beasts.
Bear with me. I am
neither sawdust doll nor brutish monk.
I wear
foolish collar, sacking
the circus pie
of a clown whose passionate will
persuades him to be useless,
whose death
sheriffs, cardinals, generals
conspire, in the old moralities
to bring to pass—
a providence, a use.

O church and state
my church, O mausoleum;
state
the stated clerk of death
I take in my two hands
the tortured mother, the blighted child
the prisoner's face
lax as a wax work—
Christ's tears have dulled
the sheriff's rage, sharpened
the doll's dead eyes.
Surprise!
(we have his word)
we burst like straw
our sexual death
we sow like autumn fools
hope in the leprous furrow.

HELP ME SOMEONE

I should like to know please
the name of that girl
lauded in some obscure corner
of the press

dead in Paris
buried in Père Lachaise cemetery,
dedicated it was said, to the common
life of man

an American girl
solicitous for the sick
succoring outcasts
showing the city of light
an unaccustomed
incandescence.

Where then?
her bones make
so small a sound
in the noiseless sockets
of history

and *learn! learn!* is the law
whereby we stand
and they
cut free.

INDEPENDENCE DAY AND AFTER

Our old Alma
battens down her hatches;
the Alumni Vets of Freedom
come for that big annual
Clan Wake—hurray!

the day when the flag
wears itself
as a peacock's brain a
gorgeous inviolate tail
    no one (by God and us)
    ever will have a piece of!

July 5; rake the scorched lawns
send up old glory again, a
shipwreck signal;

    the color bars, the tricky
    stars
    One evening light
breathes free.
The heavens
weep and laugh together
psycho and sane
for human folly

THE CHURCH IS NAMED
MOTHER OF FAIR LOVE

Panic of dark minds sounds
about the level brows, the austere skull
that harbors like a shell
the inmost mystery of all years.
Sternness, compassion in those eyes;

come near, the quick and dead. Be born of me.

SAINT FRANCIS

Sometimes
I come through
like the first note
of a trumpet
fired with morning
round as a Saturn ring
hot and cold
as a virgin's brow

highest C

off your radar your purported
ears
stuffed like mouths
with yesterday's omelettes
trussed like turkeys
groaning;
they have stolen
alas my
heart my
gizzard my
2 rare
unstrung pearls.

No; there went ME;
my heart's thrum thrum my
gizzard's auld lang syne my
pearls' sound of milk
warm from the tit, hitting
(squall) the cat's eyeball

unheard unheard as love
mostly on
Thanksgiving Christmas your
trussed capons your
burning babes.

No—
the sweet spontaneous
animals hear
me and
fear not and
draw
near.

SOMETHING ABOUT SOMEONE
NAMED YOU OR ME

He walks with his winter shadow.
He is all hoar's breath,
health; he strides, a visible
heart, the sun's hair spring.
Who calls him incomplete?

The artist does;
crossed bones, a rusted cage,
hardware, kinetics. An argument
too easily won.
     Then—
who calls him man?

I wait his death
I will touch him to a Jew.

Junk man, skies fall on you
a rain of glory, a fire fall—
new ways into the world.

VI

TRIAL POEMS

1. WINGS

In Baltimore as we flew in for trial
a butterfly   came to rest on our big
                             Boeing wing
pulsed there, a hand in ballet motion, a heartbeat.
I wished the little tacker luck.   He was
technologically innocent, flying
by grace of the US Air Control Command
because his wing-spread
(I checked this)
lay somewhere below the danger area
                            of the breadth
of minor aircraft.

2. THE MARSHAL

The marshal is taking my measure
snip   snip   snip, crossways, back and front
he X's me, society's darling, dun shirt and pants.
He grins past my shoulder
a clown head at odds with its fate.

His ribald revolver eye
(steel sights, barrel nose)
is taking my measure.
I will wear khaki (he grins) and love it
for years and years
and play
night and day
cops and robbers;
in dreams, for years
will scramble the wall like a spider,
               fall
piecemeal,
        into my savior's throttling arms.

3. JOHN UREY

In our big cruel cell block
designed like a city hospital
for the spreading of disease
I came on an old pulp sheet;
in a corner
of its rubbishy mind
the news shone; a priest who made history.
John Urey
in the Manhattan sty Dickens slogged
one hundred years after
(preserved to this day; slums being
our manifest destiny)
   'dens where dogs would howl to lie
   ruined houses open to the street—
   hideous tenements
                their names
   drawn from robbery and murder;
                        whatever is
   loathsome, drooping and decayed . . .'
The priest, in and out of an alehouse
ministered to slaves by night,
sought like a slave by the carnivore
founding fathers
             whose dentures gleam
in the old portraits, like sharks
in grand banks of privilege.

The night before our trial
opens its jaws (an old shark yawn, gold-capped
with privilege, boredom, bankruptcy),
I think of John Urey;
down the bleak corridor
Philip's typewriter,
           the stick of a blind prophet
argues the deities blind,
Tom Lewis ponders tomorrow—
from swine tending at Lewisburg prison

to Baltimore court, one scene and the same;
the parable of Jesus
keeps sane his gentle spirit. . . .

Wherefore John Urey, make common cause with us
indicted felons, for pouring of blood and fire
on murderous licenses;
lead into court
                    the great society's
everyday catch;
                    the dying children, burned, blinded
in Washington rose gardens;
give evidence upon that power
wasted like seed or life's blood
on whoring and butchery.

John Urey, tell our Father
face to face, in beatific vision
we hallowed hold His name.

4. GUILTY

Supersonic time
that noses the ether
like a hell hound
on mercy and bombing missions
bore me here
dropped me like a dud

I sit in the town stocks
for ten thousand years
a judge's or butcher's scrawl
GUILTY around my neck.

On a park bench in Japan
a man's shadow sits
after the bomb's wink
ten thousand years

until God wink again
like a lucky fisherman
and a man's mouth snap
shut   on the hook they say
God says stands for hope

The man screams or yawns
unheard from as a fish
or a man at rope's end
by Goya or Daumier

5. A TYPICAL DAY
IN THE MUNICIPAL ZOO

We sit, we walk our cage
day after day;
at night, the moon
striped like a tiger
leaps on us with a cry.

Unlikely men, white, black
sweating with rage and grief
our diet decreed
by our own prophetic guts—

the prison poems of Ho,
the sayings of Chairman Jesus.

6. EUCHARIST

7 A.M. trial day,
courtesy of Warden Foster,
the San Jose vineyards
and a common baking shop

we took
in a workman's cracked cup
at a slum table

prisoners' pot luck

7. THE BOXES OF PAPER ASH

   the size of infant caskets
were rolled in on a dolly
heaped there like cordwood
or children after a usual
air strike on Hanoi.
I heard between heartbeats
of Jesus and his hangman
the children's mouths mewing
for the breasts of murdered women
the blackened hands beating
the box of death for breath.

8. THE VERDICT

Everything before was a great lie.
Illusion, distemper, the judge's eye
Negro and Jew for rigorists,
spontaneous vengeance. The children die
singing in the furnace. They say in hell
heaven is a great lie.

                Years, years ago
my mother moves in youth. In her
I move too, to birth, to youth, to this.
The judge's *toc toc* is time's steel hand
summoning; *come priest from the priest hole. Risk!*
Everything else
is a great lie. Four walls, home, love, youth
truth untried, all, all is a great lie.
The truth the judge shuts in his two eyes.
Come Jesuit, the university cannot
no nor the universe, nor vatic Jesus
imagine. Imagine! Everything before
was a great lie.

              Philip, your freedom
stature, simplicity, the ghetto where the children
malinger, die—
            Judge Thomsen
strike, strike with a hot hammer
the hour, the truth. The truth has birth
all former truth must die. Everything
before; all faith and hope, and love itself
was a great lie.

VII

NEW POEMS

Cornell Poems

1. ARRIVAL (1967)

Left New York by Mohawk jet
 for Ithaca;
 fair trading of cities? no.
 but recalled during that flight
Pascal; *the heart has its reasons.*

 Yes. That organ
  of inmost sight and surprise
  imperated, and I came

a minor
 humorously welcomed
  species in the great think tank
 me

whom even
 crowned with his crown
  the incumbent whale
 -'s regnant eye rolls
   sidewise to see

2. A SUPPER IN MEMORY

(for Matthew Goodman, d. August 1967)

That evening I came
to a house numbered—something ½
I have forgotten the street, no longer
extant. We ate with chopsticks
the Japanese food, inexpertly.
Laughing, give and take, contrary lessons
"this way; no that" fingering the tools.
Guests; Bert in phylacteries intoning
Jewish grace, with commentary;
"give peace, we being such goddamn
fools, will not easily of ourselves
bring it to pass." Linda in sari
at the stove concocting marvels;
Her-She the dog; the big music box
like a fakir's carpetbag, huffing
sounds like exotic cobras and flowers

and Matthew in a brown study laying down
another assault on that rude Hampshire spine

To think half murmured Linda as the fire
died *we never thought to say we love him*

His glance
        dry
                sweet humored
                            free—
you must take
all the chances a good poem takes
no mountain but reads a man
the fear   the quality

He looked around
                    confident as his mountain
unwounded
            saw
what sight engenders of the world
before night—
no death
            no age
                    no betrayal
                            saw them
a full circle
            a filled vessel
                        he
Matthew
        drank

they premonitory   tasting   in the passed cup
that unbearable lack   that illest luck

3. THE GORGES

Coming opens a chasm.
I think both of the Lord's
and a woman's body; invention
(literally) by spike or rod
mothers life. Father broods
like a waylaying cloud above
waters he struck open

The university falls away forever
its gift numbs like a cataract
lisps like an undergraduate's
numbers. Choose your entailing
season, read as you run

I come like the moon
crossing the chasm, a footless midnight
trespasser on Triphammer bridge.
Indeed a feeble passage after
sun all day struck sparks like shod hooves—
intelligence, panoply of artists,
genius, entelechy.
                          The bells
make passion logical. Stone on stone
rising, water on waters pausing
falling, a law of minds;
                              above
shekinah, the glory of God
                              beneath
here and there, pools, cold, untouchable
wisdom
          the sun never
X's like doomed trees
                          for the hot
      glance of its ax

4. AUTUMN, THE STREAMS ARE HEAVY

One day; coming home
treading effortfully
(the gorges, a geography, a friendship
the years make difficult
terrain)

sudden
air   water
conjoin
I am immersed, you
shaped heaven and earth
I am nowhere safe
like a bloodlet Christ
taken
hapless in my crown
my murder,
Father.

Was, no not one
sweet reason
why men should not
like fish mouths
drink the light and
die
like fish in Christian legend,
rise
pied like rainbows from the cave

No reason!
      trees and fish
whisper like elders;
     seek
          in breaking bones the hero's springing,
   in self sacrifice
  the breathing span
   of bridges and new men—
  in night watches and sweat
     the icy lakes
    death may not sour or slake!

5. FLEW TO NEW YORK, A BAPTISM EVENT RENDERED CHANCY BY TRAVEL RESTRICTIONS OF THE U. S. PROSECUTOR

Returned, unapprehended.

time and purpose unscathed;
home. On the sink drainboard
a scrawled note; "Missed you again,
you were off I suppose, preaching liberation."
(A spring flower placed carefully atop the note)
"The cookies are fabulous. See you soon."

> (Cleveland Sellers, black, 5 year sentence for
> refusal of hunting privileges
> in the Man's preserve. He smiles as though
> the game's outcome were (it is) in his own hands.)

I should stare upon the dead or go back
long and long, to a hideous jail, or return to the womb of
                                              my mother
in order
to understand, stand under—

So took up the flower, common as our fate, tomorrow's
discard. Filled a stem glass,
placed the flower, a prima donna, in a box seat.
Let tomorrow wane. The flower
blooms like Tolstoi's ripe riposte,
                              her naked shoulders
taking time in stride,
                    one white wing, then another.

6. CRISIS: POISON IN THE IVY

Today six elderly mandarins, resorting to the N. Y. Times
          (that last infirmary of grey minds),
               proclaim: Academic Freedom Still Exists At Cornell.
They quote Socrates to no purpose; like Homer's old men
manning the battlements, a buzzing of locusts.
Their lives like this; descent like bald outmoded deities on wires
from segregated heavens. They befoul the dust
   with this or that exhausted tradition,
      ascend again, out of sight and mind
     the heavens closing like a trap. Requiescat!

         Everything said and done! in S.D.S. heads
           sanity scrambles like eggs,
              the big graffiti on construction fences
      melt overnight, an op nightmare.
         Insolvency, despairing wit. Students busted
  (an image of rag dolls, cops breaking like dry sticks
       Jehovah's cunning handiwork)

       The ivy frets and crawls like poison ivy
         infecting the solid battlements of mind
     breaking that Hanseatic league to bits.
        O John Harvard, Messrs Brown and Yale
   original sin, your transplant rottens the commonwealth
       Ezra Cornell turns watery where he stands
        his land grant sours, his piracies
     bring in no cash. O foundering father!

7. THE PHILOSOPHY OF THE AGRICULTURAL SCHOOL IS HEREBY QUESTIONED IF NOT CHALLENGED

Lo the world
    corruptive, generative
        as a sow's underbelly—

men long to reify their lives
        a continent
  in the sea's discontent

           Farmer John at the fence
           seeing that tipped, carnal, teeming
           sea; a hive, a porcine
           golden goose—

Nevertheless.   *John,* warns pig admonitory—
        hang loose

8. PRES. CORSON DECLARES
THE UNIVERSITY VALUE FREE.
SOME OF US DEMUR

Some insane wall eyed general
A god or goose in stiff britches
goose steps like god down Wall Eye Street
crossing at Blue As Hell. He looms bigger.
He totes a courier bag of infant heads
like hearts of artichoke, the income tax
thrust at him by abortive obedient cits.
Doors open and slam, regurgitate like jaws
jews, damages, hooks and eyes, indentures.

I watch like a Milano cop on the Day of Kings
or Jesus strapped in hell to a rich man's bed.
The loot piles up around. Hark the
herald! Dow Chemical warms
with elegant piss the icy straw. A hand
discreet as a publican's on a whore's thigh
warms
the cockles of my wax, wan and sacred
heart.

Certain Events, No Connection with Cornell, So to Speak

1. TO A SOLDIER, SLEEPING IN AN AIRPORT WAITING ROOM
(after the Pentagon)

I prayed as I went past—
his thought might flow
gentle as water, lax from his hands
languishing in no
five-sided hell,
the labyrinthe
we sat in
like clubbed watch dogs
two weeks before.

No D.C. nightmare, soldier.
O that the sleep
were wakening, the innocent inwardness
yours for good!
wasps from a hive
the troops poured out, a seventh plague
from the porticoes. Sleep on—
take oath to sleep, the Pentagon
doth murder sleep! under the brute flares
they hustled us, harmless as flies
into the spider's parlor.

Dreams strip you
like a bride's handmaids
of filth of office,
hire you out

to no one's whoring power. Your body's
fratricidal steel
plunge like a lover's tool into the fire
where lust forgets its fury,
the plowshares
like Sunday dolphins play
earth, sea,
for all their worth and birth.

2. WADING AT SIX-MILE CREEK: LENT, BLOOD AND NO TEARS; 1969

My favorite lower case
anti idol
whom modest talk
and courage, that fathering virtue
touch,

(How's that for invocation?)

I put on my second best socks
like the latest incarnation
its memories, ribs and holes
(Argentina wove them when I
for making love not war
was kicked by a sacred war horse and
went flying south like a carpet)

Alas and hooray. Here and now
I put on my socks
along 6 mile creek
(polluted, rambunctious)
drawing
March 23, the icicle from my heart's well
to record

Spring!—
good friends
made bloody shambles
last night in D.C.
of Dow Chemical.
They sprayed that abattoir
with blood,
enraged
the tonsorially impeccable
mass killers
righteous as hangmen

their white hands reeking
(the children following
transfigured, a cloud of furies). . . .

When you open the testament, you risk
(I was saying yesterday
to empty air)
risk all hell.
Like pulling a plant
by its roots, leeks or carrots—
the plant bleeds; it is man, you
hold by the hair
disembodied, a human head—speak!

or you open the book
(my friends, my friends, fasting, in jail)
you cast a match in a tinder
It flares!
you will lose your sight; you will
go mad or blind.

Blood and napalm; the book,
remember, danger!

3. DEATH OF A DEER

Impaled
in big mindless lights
he touched heels to us
as a drumming stick its head

then arched away
folding his legs
like the elbows of a drummer
pausing—
a split second late!
we broke that beat, that heart—
threw him
headlong into the shark jaws
of a hurtling Buick

he lay
bloody as birth, the wet head
just born
          beyond—
nostrils, eyes, mouth
roped with blood, the tragic essence
of our air, when the innocent
breathe, and bleed for it

It was war time, our Volkswagen
thin as eggshell; we stood there
he died there, trailing
the fouled life line; guts
genitals, spreadeagled.
the unanswerable eyes
of a murdered child, the dun
peasant rags
night flares

and cold as ikons or iconoclasts, the
savage sophisticated gods,
our fun done
        helpless
as the dead
to resurrect

4. IN EXALTATION OF SO SIMPLE A THING, AN AUTUMN TREE

Has not let blood
nor lied in his teeth
nor made mock
nor defrauded
nor worshipped idols
nor extinguished truth

But
like anemone
or a golden fish—
blushes, pales at the nearing
bridegroom
whom you (we)
in fear-ridden
vocables
flee
crying

reality!

5. THE SERMON ON THE MOUNT, AND THE WAR THAT WILL NOT END FOREVER

Jesus came down from Crough Patrick
crazy with cold, starry with vision.
The sun undid what the moon did; unlocked him.

Light headed ecstasy; *love*
he commended, as tongue and teeth
fixed on it; *love* for meat after fast;

then *poverty*, &
mild and clean hearts stood commended.

Next spring, mounted Crough Patrick
and perished.
The word came down
comes down and down, comes what he said

men say, gainsy, say nay.

Not easy for those who man
the mountain, forever ringed and fired.
And the children, the children
                                    die
die like our last chance
                    day
                            after Christian day

6. 1879—MY FATHER—1969

90 bawling years, then you died off
        your skinny face puffed out
        yellow as a mandarin's
        your mouth pursed
        your head rolled slightly aside
        (a fallen fruit under a shift of frost.)

You; your poetry gushing
        ream after worthless ream
        out of leaky tear ducts
you; breaking clods years and years
        a farm horse
        strapped to the old farm horse.

Then your jaw dropped, a semaphore
        the last train out of ghost town.
        in 2 brown sacks
        we gathered everything you owned,
                an immigrant's or pauper's bundle

I leaned over the bed, breathing for you
        all that night long
        (somebody else leaned over too)
        2 shadows over a fish tank
        Helpless as sons or fathers
                watching the death
        of the fish from whom
        all men, fathers and sons
        ad infinitum come;
        A fish metamorphosing
        into a father before our eyes—

I could not take you in my arms, give you back
        wits, volatile energy
        confounding moods, appetite
        the farm, drought, depression years
        the scythe that whistled
        like a wood plane across hard earth—

did you want it back, anyway?
    Think. 6 sons, 5, 4, 3, 2, 1—
    then zero, a wedding night, a bride,
    the thing awaiting doing all again. . . .

You hated like all hell that necessity
    we lived by—your scant love.
    On each of us, the stigmata
    took years to heal; making do,
    improvisations, wrong turns,
    fear, damnation, fury.

Well, we made it; some deep root of sanity
    we sucked on. Above, small town hear
    the thrashing storms you created,
    chaos your element.

Sanity too; your face, dropping its mask
    asleep over a book;
    Irish intelligence; now and again
    a piercing stab of virtue; a boy
    kneeling beside you at Mass, a 6 yr. old
    rocking horse Catholic.

    Thank you, old bones, old pirate,
    old mocker and weeper.

You could have lived to a hundred. But contrary
passion set in, *horror vacui;* falling
downstairs that last time, into your own
depths. *To hell with it, bag it all!*
A bloody act of the will,
a fever nursed by rage. Sons
were no longer mitigating presences, who
now and again, had been.

We; has been now. You turned to the wall

I write this, a mad airport interlude
mad equinox, mad Jersey;
catapults, bulldozers
shack privies, macadam, earth works—
Father, they are grinding the sweet land
to absolute death.
We are bombed back to the stone age.
No recourse, except—
hatred and love, your hand,
its arm breaking through earth
nightmare or miracle;
Your face muffled in its shroud,
disdaining
the folly nailing
us here
at high polluted tide
like stinking fish
ancestors, sons, nailed
to the world's botched cross.

In Memoriam; Thomas Merton

1. 1969 OPENED LIKE THIS

I wish I had some joy—
the text of eyes that pay
this year, all the last exacted; tears.
When Merton died, we met, struck dumb,
the old year's locking jaw
let blood, one last time; death, then this death.

We blow up big the photo Griffin made
Kentucky woods, hunched arms
overalls, Picasso moon face. Eyes

like a wrapt stranger among mourners
on a road, of a noon, in a landscape
stinking like graves. Hands outstretched
    filled with this world's
        (no other's)
           flowers, wounds;
              I have some joy!

2. AT THE TIME OF HIS DEATH, AMERICANS HAD MASTERED THE DYNAMICS OF A MOON FLIGHT

Merton's gone; that comfort ended.
The moon, bleak as an earth, blinks
bad cess back to us. That comfort
          when free as promises or willows
          or the future
          the moon hung there
          and all hands lifted
          like priests or brides
          brides or
          (minded and ringed)
          geese, straining, crying
          a northern tongue—

          ended

3. EDIFYING ANECDOTES CONCERNING THE DECEASED ARE NOW IN ORDER

January; a sick woman
garnished with the dumb potatoes
of average do-gooders
preserved, propped there
a vinyl-sprayed op exhibit;
Soup Cans, Groceries; "IDEAL SLUM."
(Around her hideous fairy tales arise
in the eyes of the children of good parents
potato parents, canned pops and moms)

Enter Merton.
He stooped and kissed the woman
(she dying not of this ill or that
but of all   all
her life and ours)
offered
six roses
A sudden weeping seized her
drained by average goodness of church and state
their boiled eyes and lives.

Touché, excelling man!
never again shall we
(canned, mashed, boiled
in the short order of creation)
cry out, exult—never again
that rite of roses
that rightness, the rose that leaps
once, and for all
dies

4. MEMORIES AFTER THE FACT:
A VISIT OF ILL-FAVORED CHARACTERS
TO THE MONASTERY

Under the stars, a last beer
cans flipped in the underbrush
good night, good night . . .

Friend, between Bangkok and this
new year zeroing in, how death
abounds, for those who try and try

the odds you took and tossed, on life!
Coffee and hamburg in a Greek hash joint
alone; a Bogie double feature. Winds stir

dead news in the street, frenzy, bombast. Meat
sticks in my throat. The gravel voice
of dead Bogart

cheats like a virtuous thief
usurious times.
Merton, of all who tremble and tear

sheets from their calendars
or shroud in nightmare
the whelmed dead to their eyes

you and I—

(The old men loom, their winter agon
nearing the newborn.
The bony fingers point, appoint

our eschaton and his; death, prison and
good night, good night.)

5. WHO'S WHO AT THE OBSEQUIES

General Hershey did not mourn
you, nor Roy Harris nor
Cleaver's hell's angels.
The sombre Texan war lord
braved New York crazies
to shed
a vagrant tear
on a cardinal's pall—
he minded this day
his waning power and war.
Et Cetera bought farms
or oxen
or took wives
the day your death
shook the earth's round

Only the raped and rent
the shadowed, submerged
upon whom Kafka's needles
bear down, write large
the cuneiform of loss—

were there. And the four
ministering spirits of these;
earth, water, fire, air.

6. THE FUNERAL ORATION
AS PRONOUNCED BY
THE COMPASSIONATE BUDDHA

Assembled sirs. The courtesies afforded us by the Dali Lama,
the Abbot of the Trappist Fathers
and the vergers of your cathedral, are deeply felt
and enter as a sombre joy into our heart's stream.

The Christ himself (to whom all praise) were better chosen
to speak for this monk, brother and son.
Alas. The absence of your god, decreed by a thousand
    malevolencies
susurration, anger, skill in summoning his words against him—
I hear your choice, approving; *one god at a time. Better an
    unknown god, even*
a tedious one, than that holy son, native to our flesh.
Better a subtle millennial smile, than anger and infected wounds.
Better me than he. So be it; I shall speak.

The assumption of this monk into ecstasy,
the opening of the crystal portals before that glancing spirit!
He was (I speak a high and rare praise)
not too strenuous after reward; so he attains eternal knowledge.
In his mortal journey, he refused direction from those pylons
impermeable, deadly smooth,
hard to the touch as the membrane of hell.
He detested their claim upon the soul, he exorcised their rumors.

(I too have been a guest in your cities. I have been conducted with
    pomp
through your martian workshops, heard with a start of fear
the incantations of your genius.
Indeed the aim is clear; saints, the innocent, visionaries,
all targets of your encompassing death wish.

But the Buddha knows no disdain; he stoops low to enter your
     labyrinth,
to uncoil its secret, to bare its beast.
The Buddha, a length of rope, a dog in the dust; such parables I
     embrace
once more, in tribute to this monk.)

The monk has attained god;
he had first attained man. Does the nexus trouble you, issuing as it
     does
from a mouth so neutral, so silent as mine? Be comforted.
Gioconda exists only to smile. She does so; her value mounts and
     mounts.

But the monk Merton, in his life and going forth
requires that a blow be dealt
your confident myths. If the gods are silent
if even to this hour, Christ and Buddha stand appalled
before your idols, if we breathe the stench of your hecatombs—
still, the passage of a good man restores;
it brings the gods to earth, even to you!
For once, for a brief space, we walk among you
for a space of words,
we quicken your hearts in pursuit of the sovereign will.
O makers and unmakers! I shall shortly be borne
in a flowering cart of sandal, into high heaven; a quaint apotheosis!
The routine slaveries once more possess you.
Man and god, Buddha and Merton, those years, this hour, fold in like
     a dough.
The blows of the kneading fist withdraw, the times are your own.
War readying of war;
conflicts, games of death, checks and counters—
I leave you, your undoing, promethean doers and despoilers.

Hope?
Christ and Buddha fashion a conundrum. Hear it.
The hour of your despoiling is the hour of our return.

Until then, the world is yours, and you are Moloch's, bound hand
    and foot
upon a wheel of fire.

The monk Thomas I take up in lotus hands
to place in the eternal thought
a jewel upon my forehead.

From the Underside

1. ANNOUNCEMENT

Thursday a week, all weather forbidding
Sunday, or at any rate, Friday
Bess Truman, Mamie, Mrs. Onassis, Ladybird and Pat
will assemble for a Women's Lib rap at Ellis Island.
Beginning with the beautification thing
to wit, the cloaking of a sunk oil derrick
the planting of a two-day-old redwood in Assassination Plaza.
And on then to the main event,
the obliteration of the obscene graffiti legible to this day
at that Lady's libertarian feet.
Causative also of one hundred years of rude snickers
from the curious mouths of Wops, Frogs, Micks, Jewboys, Spiks
and the unmentionable riff-raff dumped on our shores from nigger
    slaveholds.
You recall; "Come to me ye despised."
Each in turn, then in vigorous unison, the First Lady and the
    Former F.L.'s
will scrub and scrub and scrub.
Ladies rub it out.
Then if you can prevail on that foggy Cassandra,
that brazen-lipped Mona Lisa, to lower in reality's name her sleeve
    of fire,
take off her crown of thorns,
unstring the lights that brought, truth told, like Circe's maiden
    swine,
ships and their men innumerable to ruin.
Topple her, sell her metal for smelting of a new cannon   senator
    whore.

2. I WILL SIGN MY NAME

Now what the hell sort of dog's life is left to limp?
I may not mean what I see.
The FBI has devised for this emergency a poetry censor
whose eyes flame like an alcoholic's,
         smoke like Beelzebub's dry ice or dry armpit
when the bubonic smell of a poetic name-place
         falls under its snub snout.
I may not name river.
No, nor mountain, street   alley nor valley.
At least I will sign my name.
Now hold your nose, eyes, ears,
         in a one-mile perimeter of infernal headquarters.
All hell will shortly like dull scissors and sirens
         gouge, saw, at the inner ear.
Ready? Set? Then.
         Daniel Berrigan.

3. QUESTION AND ANSWER

Query: Shall a man then return
         to the womb of his mother, reborn?
Jesus: As you said: earth, old basket-born, hard-beaked hen
         wants you for egg.
No, I hereby (he scrawled on the inside of his shell)
attest to my first
         Will and Testament.
I shall go forth bare-assed as a new moon,
         stellar as baby Jesus.
Everyone's sight and scandal. Yes and No.
And the vast milky way perhaps between.

4. THE THREE GODS VISIT THE EARTH AND FIND IT WANTING

I might be one of those gods in the old Zen tales or the testament,
pro tempore reduced in circumstances, wandering the earth.
Benign curiosity, the ebb and flow of destiny,
anxious too not to lose touch.
How are men faring?
I would sit at their evening leeks and Sin Foo tea
inquire about harvest, children
   whatever seemed germane to that place.
Then thanks, farewell at the door. And presto, apotheosis.
Slightly elevated, my form set free from the base earth,
I would bless them, household, bloodline
   with classical phrase.
My head bathed in a blaze,
   a saint's head in a rococo cupola painting.
To wit; *may the pitcher never fail your thirst,*
   your grape vine wither,
eternal life to boot!
They kneeling there bowed, Bavarian figurines. . . .
Ah, in any case, no.
Wonder workers are dead as doornails, rococo painters and popes.
Jesus included.
If that Jew lives at all
   he lives at the edge,
overlooked by the swath of the cutting scythe.
If in me; an animal
   whose pelt a rough weapon would damage;
Bring him in through guile, a rare enough specimen.
If in my friends; day-to-day improvising, harassment,
   brows burning with political fevers
under duress too; warned of harboring, aiding, abetting.
I come and go. Friends pass. Gratitude heavy as death on my
     tongue.
They and I unconsoled.
   Up, up the killing slope, no cover, no relief.
The century.

5. THE DIVINE IDEA

That divine idea Jesus cooked up in his Cordon Bleu intellect!
Well, I would like to ask something
    of the Deity's privileged cuisinier
or his disciples, numberless as stars. Or christian people.
Where do you turn, pray, when the sleek doberman packs
    cover the waterfront
and Cagneys, Bogeys, Tracys, sell out to law and order?
And the Cordon Bleu chef whets knife on the emory
and twelve gourmets are seated in the cathedral nave,
starved as race horses or bridegrooms?
Assize lifts like a starting gate, falls like a bride's last veil.
Enter, on trenchers, the pièce de résistance.
    You guessed it.

6. A PROFFER

Look; a proffer slipped into the molars
   of G. Washington's portrait
that mouth a mail slot
   for the double agent doubling back.
Dear coon-hunters and hounds;
by the full moon I swear
if you bring home our boys (say, on the hour)
if you order in-shore all oil boats, freeze off-shore rigs,
if you dismantle the silos,
settle generals and generals' wives
   in perpetual-care nudist camps,
if you indemnify the exhausted earth
   for its false labor pains
I hereby pledge;
   will live and die, abiding law,
reincarnate as an FBI coon-dog
   whistle, moon, wife, whatever.

7. RIVER

My little friend a flutist sits far side of the river
one knee drawn up, accoutred like Pan.
Past him and me, cries of the oarsmen, knifing prows
   shells headlong as hounds.
Over his head a natural outcropping,
willow fronds leap as though music were natural urgings, spark in
    the vein.
To a first glance everything is in perfect order.
All has been celebrated before, coherent, dutiful.

Never believe it.
He plays on a human thigh bone veined with blood.
There is blood on his hands, venery and stealth in eyes.
Nine-tenths of the somnolent sun-gazers at ease here
   will, truth known,
hand me over to judgment.
The big flag above, all but blots out the sun.
A folly. A whore's hips.
The mercy I grasp is
   only partially to grasp
   this noon nightmare,
nightshade held to my lips.

8. WARNING

Mind must learn to go like cat's or crow's feet
blending with near cover.
Manifest destiny makes mincemeat of mice.
Short work of.
I spit on my hands like a raccoon,
    say my prayers like a hunched baboon,
begging the man whose shoulder carries
    sunrise, umbrellas, crosses, me;
Make me a mind the wise man bears
    like unto all things, common earth to angel.
Grant me cover, sweet Christ, the coney crieth;
Strike blank all those mug shots the hunter beareth.

9. ON BEING HERE WITH PHIL

5/29/71

Whenever I met a crook here
    (con man, forger, break and entry, stocks and bonds)
I think gratefully
    as we pump damp hands
of Uncle Sam.

Strangely also of that dancing bear
who used on command
to heave himself up on slack legs
and flog about, an obscene pandemonium
like 5 men in a bear suit
up and down, rue Madame
in Paris, in '64.

Every day the gypsies would lead him out
chained at the neck
in a different scrap of costume—
a gypsy, a drunk, a clown
tatterdemalion, his rags tossed on him
    that A.M.
from ash cans or the Paris dump.

One and the same act, same moth-eaten bear.
You could see, if you wished to see
under the mask, the battered stovepipe hat
the fathomless liquid eyes, devoid
of terror or spirit. Eyes of a winded old horse
a cancer patient, a befuddled gypsy, a prisoner.

This is what makes of pity a useful virtue.
I pump hands with the latest middle-age crook.
He played dominoes with Uncle Sam and lost.
Everyone loses: Rather—a sufficient number of suckers
to keep the game dangerous
with public display of captive bears.

This one will dance here, 9 months or a year, a chain
dangling from his neck. (Lt. Strychnine
calling the dance) clothed like an animal
from the US Army dump.
Some call it eating crow.

The crows laze overhead
like debris from the industry stack.
Day and night for slave wages
the prisoners make war instruments
to drop on Vietnamese peasants. This integrates
captive bears
with the "national effort."
The local shrinks in government hire
urge the prisoners into the factory
with psychological cattle prods.
Early parole is the reward
for bears who dance
as though their foot pads smoked
on hot coals.

The diet is crow.
Some go mad of it
One prisoner broke his chain
Climbed the water tower
befuddled, trying to catch crow
on the wing. Fellow bears
bellowed
obscene encouragement; jump you motherfucker

Sometimes (rarely, once or twice) pumping hands
with this or that crook, you see
flash out
not that old sodden look of defeat
but the game, the click, the authentic old
killer himself

the eyes of Uncle Sam.
(This is what makes of anger a useful virtue)
200 years old, about to celebrate
the bicentenary of his revolution.
The look of a war poster;
Uncle Sam Wants You.

You're damned right he does.
The look goes through my body like a needle.
This one is no loser. This one
is light on his feet. The Russian bear
is yesterday's cub compared with this one.
Compared with this one
Your kind is practically extinct.
As to the future, any future
prisoners are advised to (do)
consult this one.

10. TULIPS IN THE PRISON YARD

All kinds of poets, believe me, could better praise your
    sovereign beauty, your altogether subtle translation
        of blank nature
                So that winds, night, sunlight
    (extraordinarily colorless phenomena) are drawn into
What can only be called a "new game." Well I will not revel
    in humiliation. Yeats, Wordsworth, would have looked once
Breathed deeply, gone home, sharpened quills,
        with a flourish plucked you from time.
        But
        You are jailyard blooms, you wear bravery with a
                                  difference
    You are born here, will die here. Making you, by excess of
                               suffering
And transfiguration of suffering, ours.
                I see prisoners pass
In the dead spur of spring, before you show face.
                Are you their glancing tears
The faces of wives and children,
                the yin yang of hearts
To-fro like hanged necks,
                in perpetual cruelty, absurdity?
The prisoners
Pass and pass, shades of men, pre-men, khaki ghosts; shame,
                              futility.
Between smiles, between reason for smiles, between
    Life as fool's pace and life as celebrant's flame, is
        Aeons.
    Yet—thank you. Against the whips
        of ignorant furies, the slavish pieties of Judas priests
You stand, a first flicker in the brain's soil, a precursor
    of judgment—

Dawn might be
Man may be
Or spelling it out in the hand's palm
of a blind mute;
God is fire
is love.